Bilingual
Guide
to Japan

SAMURAI CASTLES

MIURA Masayuki

English Text by Chris Glenn

SHOGAKUKAN

Bilingual Guide to Japan
SAMURAI CASTLES
Second edition

MIURA Masayuki
English Text by Chris Glenn

Book and Cover Design © Kindaichi Design
English Text © Chris Glenn

Published by
SHOGAKUKAN
2-3-1 Hitotsubashi Chiyoda-Ku,
Tokyo 101-8001 JAPAN
http://www.shogakukan.co.jp
https://japanesebooks.jp/en

All rights reserved.
No part of this publication may be reproduced in any form or by any means, graphic, electronic or mechanical, including photocopying and recording by an information storage and retrieval system, without written permission from the publisher.

This book is the second new edition of
SHIRO BILINGUAL GUIDE by
MIURA Masayuki, Chris Glenn
© 2019 MIURA Masayuki, Chris Glenn,
UCHIDA Kazuhiro / SHOGAKUKAN
Printed in Japan
ISBN 978-4-09-388746-5

城バイリンガルガイド
改訂版

三浦正幸 監修

クリス　グレン　英文

小学館

English Renderings of Castle Terms

This English and Japanese bilingual book introduces the basic knowledge and representative types of *shiro* (Japanese castle).
❖ indicates World Heritage Site
◉ indicates National Treasure of Japan
Japanese unique terms are rendered in Italicized Roman characters. The only diacritical mark used in indispensable cases is the hyphen (-), to separate two adjacent vowel sounds or polysyllables.
Names of historical characters are written in English in the same order as they appear in Japanese, with family name followed by given name.

Since the conventions for rendering these terms into English differ depending on the facility, terms used elsewhere may not be consistent with those used in this book. Given that even Japanese names and pronunciations may differ depending on the region, they cannot be generalized. Standard names are used in this book and are rendered so that they can be easily read by individuals who are not native speakers of Japanese.

本書の英文表記について
この本は、代表的な城について紹介しています。日本語が母語ではない人のために、英語で記してあります。❖は世界遺産、◉は天守が国宝を表しています。
日本語はローマ字読みにし、斜体のアルファベットで表記しています。英語者が発音しにくいものには、ハイフン（-）を使用しています。

※これら外国語表記は、施設（公共施設、地方自治体等）ごとに異なるルールで表記されているため、本書と一致しない場合があります。特に城の部分名称とその発音については、地方によって日本語でも呼び方が異なることがあり、一般化はできません。本書では標準的な呼称を掲載し、外国語を母語とする読者ができるだけ平易に発音できる表記としました。

Table of Contents 目次

Introduction 6　はじめに

Chapter 1　第一章
Building a Castle　城のつくり方

Shirotori 10　Nawabari 12　城取　縄張
Hori and Dorui 14　Ishigaki 16　堀と土塁　石垣
The Structure of Ishigaki 18　石垣の構造
Curvature and Gradients of Ishigaki 20　石垣の反りと勾配
Yokoya 22　Kabe and Hei 24　横矢　壁と塀
Sama and Ishi-otoshi 26　Jomon 28　狭間と石落　城門
Masugata 30　Yagura 32　枡形　櫓
The Many Names of Yagura 34　Tenshu 36　櫓の名称　天守
Inside the Tenshu 38　Goten 40　Tei-en 42　天守の内部　御殿　庭園
Joka-machi 43　Samurai-yashiki 44　城下町　侍屋敷

Chapter 2　第二章
History of Castles　城の歴史

Yayoi–Heian Period 48　弥生時代〜平安時代
Kamakura–Early Muromachi Period 49　鎌倉時代〜室町時代前期
Late Muromachi Period 50　室町時代後期（戦国時代）
Castles of the Rulers 53　Azuchi Castle 54　天下人の城　安土城
Osaka Castle 58　Edo Castle 62　大坂城　江戸城
Nagoya Castle 66　Nijo Castle 70　名古屋城　二条城
Himeji Castle 74　Matsue Castle 80　姫路城　松江城
Goryokaku 82　五稜郭

Chapter 3　第三章
Visiting Samurai Castles　名城をめぐる

Hirosaki Castle 86　Matsumoto Castle 88　弘前城　松本城
Kanazawa Castle 90　Inuyama Castle 92　金沢城　犬山城
Hikone Castle 94　Okayama Castle 96　彦根城　岡山城
Hiroshima Castle 98　Marugame Castle 99　広島城　丸亀城
Kochi Castle 100　Uwajima Castle 101　高知城　宇和島城
Iyo Matsuyama Castle 102　伊予松山城
Nakijin Gusuku 103　今帰仁城

Appendix　付録
Glossary 106　用語集
Shiro-Matsuri Festivals to Visit　訪ねてみたい城祭り
Spring 118　Summer 122　春　夏
Autumn 124　Winter 125　秋　冬

Introduction: The Unique Character of Japanese Castles

Japanese castles——not for the protection of the city

Japanese castles are divided into three periods: ancient (late 7th through 10th century), medieval (early 14th to mid-16th century), and early modern (late 16th to mid-19th century, see Azuchi-Momoyama period, p. 106). The castles of ancient Japan were often built as national enterprises. In western Japan, they were constructed for national defense against anticipated invasions from the Silla and Tang; in eastern Japan, they were militarized government offices made to allow the imperial court to suppress and rule northeastern Japan. The castles of the medieval age were built by lesser regional lords to defend their territory, and so were often smaller castles atop mountains. However, when most Japanese people think "castle," they imagine the castles of the early modern age. These castles were grand in scale and built by *daimyo* (p. 106) or the shogun. This text describes castles of the early modern period.

Many modern Japanese cities grew out of the castle towns surrounding the early modern period castles. Generally speaking, the towns where the townsfolk lived were not surrounded by castle walls; the castle was there to protect only its lord, his retainers, and their families. Battles in Japan were between

はじめに——日本の城の特色
●日本の城は都市を守るものではない
　日本の城は、古代（7世紀後期〜10世紀）、中世（14世紀初期〜16世紀中期）、近世（16世紀後期〜19世紀中期、安土桃山時代含むp. 106）の3期に分けられる。古代の城は、国家的な事業として築かれたものが多く、西日本では唐（中国）・新羅（朝鮮）からの侵略を想定した国防のための城、東日本では東北地方を朝廷が制圧して統治するための武装した役所であった。中世の城は、地方の中小領主が自己の領地を守るために築いたもので、山の上の小さな城が多かった。日本人が一般的に「城」と考えているのは、近世の城であって、将軍や大名（p. 106）が築いた大規模な城である。本書では、日本の近世の城の解説をする。
　日本の現代都市の多くは、近世の城を囲む城下町から発展した。一般的に日本で

lords, and commoners were rarely the subject of direct attack. In Europe, Korea, and China, castle walls surrounded cities to defend people from attack by foreign states. This made their castle construction techniques fundamentally different from those of Japan.

Built for an earthquake-prone nation
The castles of early modern Japan were built with *ishigaki* (stone walls) and *dorui* (earthen rampart walls) foundations, and wooden superstructures. One of the most notable characteristics of Japanese castles is how the materials used to construct the foundations and the structures were completely different. Japanese weaponry included matchlock guns, bows, spears, and swords, but cannons were hardly used at all. This meant that there was no need for sturdy materials like stone or brick when building the superstructure, as in European castles. Also, brick or stone houses are dangerous and fall easily in an earthquake-prone country like Japan.

Owing to these many earthquakes, Japanese *ishigaki* were built on gentler slopes than those of Europe or China. Similarly, because of quakes, mortar was not used in *ishigaki* construction,

は、市民が住む都市を城壁で囲まず、城は城主とその家臣や家族だけを守るものだった。日本における戦いは、城主どうしの争いだったので、市民が直接の攻撃対象ではなかったからだ。ヨーロッパや中国・朝鮮では、外国の侵略から市民を守るために城壁が都市を囲んでいたので、城の構造は日本とは根本的に異なる。
●地震多発国ならではの造り
　近世の日本の城は、基礎が石垣や土塁で築かれ、上部構造は木造建築である。基礎と上部構造で建材がまったく異なるのが日本の城の特色である。日本の武器は、鉄砲と弓矢、槍と刀であって、大砲がほとんど使われなかったため、ヨーロッパの城のように上部構造を石やレンガで頑丈に造る必要がなかった。また、地震の多い日本では、石やレンガの家は崩れやすくて危険であった。
　日本では地震に備えて、ヨーロッパや中国に比べて石垣は勾配が緩い。石を接着

the huge rocks were carefully stacked together. Though the inner precincts of the castle generally featured *ishigaki*, the castle periphery often consisted of *dorui* to save stones.

Works of art expressing the authority of the castle's lord
Notable amongst the castle's many structures were the towering *tenshu*, symbols of a lord's authority, *yagura* and *jomon*, for the defense of the castle, the *goten* where the lord resided, and other structures. Unfortunately, the majority of these wooden buildings were lost come the modern era. After World War II, the *tenshu*, symbolic of many castles, were recreated using concrete.

Though the castles of early modern Japan were military facilities, very few of them actually saw service in combat. This is because many castles were built after Japan had entered an era of peace. Consequently, a beautiful appearance and a show of the lord's authority was deemed more important than military strength. The castles of Japan provide us with powerful demonstrations of their lords' character, and for their rich creativity can be called works of art.

Masayuki Miura, Doctor of Engineering,
Emeritus Professor, Hiroshima University

するセメントがなかったので、石垣は大きな石を積み上げた構造である。一般的に城の中心部には石垣が使われるが、周辺部は石材を節約するために土塁となる。
●城主の権威を示す芸術作品
　上部構造である木造建築には、城主の権威を象徴する高層の天守、防備のための櫓と城門、城主が住む御殿などがあったが、近代になって木造建築の大部分が失われてしまった。太平洋戦争後に城の象徴である天守をコンクリートで再建した城が多い。近世の日本の城は軍事施設ではあるが、実際の戦争にほとんど使われたことがない。多くの城は平和な時代になってから築かれたからである。したがって、軍事的な強さよりも外観を美しく造って城主の権威を示すことのほうが重要であった。日本の城は、城主の個性が強く表れており、創造力に満ちた芸術作品とも言える。
（広島大学名誉教授、工学博士　三浦正幸）

Chapter 1

Building a Castle

第一章

城のつくり方

Shirotori (Castle Positioning and Construction)

Deciding where to position a castle and the planning required to construct it is known as the art of *shirotori*. Firstly, tactical requirements must be considered, such as size, how strategically important an area you need to defend, and how many men you have to defend it with. An easy-to-defend position with views of the entire area is vital to monitor traffic along strategic routes and points. Construction costs must also be taken into account. An effective castle must be authoritative and intimidating to deter invasion.

The three basic castle categories are: *yamajiro*, *hirayama-jiro* and *hirajiro*. *Yamajiro* are built on mountains, *hirayama-jiro* are situated on low hills with flatlands, and *hirajiro* are built on plains. Most castles of the medieval ages (Kamakura and Muromachi periods) were *yamajiro*, with the *kyokan* (lord's residence) located below the mountain. *Hirayama-jiro* are built on hills and incorporate the surrounding plains. *Yamajiro* and *hirayama-jiro* are not clearly defined by altitude, but by point of view. Most *hirajiro*, built on plains, appeared from the Azuchi-Momoyama period on.

These notable changes in location depended on samurai numbers. Small to medium ranked lords of the medieval ages had

城取

城を築くことを城取という。どのような場所に陣地を取るかを決めることが城づくりの第一歩だ。まず大きく見れば、領国全体に目が届くような交通の要衝に城を築くことが重要だ。立地による城の分類は大きく分けて山城、平山城、平城の3種ある。山城は山や丘の頂部付近を利用して築かれた城。中世（鎌倉時代～室町時代）に築かれた城のほとんどは山城で、城主の居館は麓に造られた。平山城は低い山や丘陵に築かれた城で、周囲の平地も利用する。山城と平山城は標高による厳密な区分はない。平城は平地に造られた城で、安土桃山時代以降に多く造られた。

城の立地の変化は、城兵の収容能力と関係する。中世は中小の領主が各自に城をもち、兵力は数十人という規模が多かった。山城は自然の地形を巧みに利用すれ

appropriately scaled castles, often with a force of only a few dozen troops. Hence *yamajiro* were built, which, through clever use of the terrain, required less engineering work reducing the economic burden.

By the Azuchi-Momoyama period, many *daimyo* found themselves governing vast territories with several hundreds of men at their service. Larger, more impressive castles with room to accommodate bigger armies were created. Instead of mountaintops, *hirayama-jiro* and *hirajiro* emerged. *Hirayama-jiro* hilltops reinforced with *ishigaki* (p. 16) provided views of the area and the *tenshu* (p. 36), and *yagura* (p. 32) looked impressive from the *joka-machi* (p. 43) and surrounding districts. Ideally, castles combined the strength and defensive capabilities of a *yamajiro* with the capacity of a *hirajiro*. In areas where an adequate mountain or hill was unavailable, *hirajiro* were constructed. Lacking natural defenses used by *yamajiro* and *hirayama-jiro*, protective and defensive structures such as wide *hori* and *dorui* (p. 14) or *ishigaki*, *yagura* and *jomon* (p. 28) were made.

ば大きな土木工事が必要ないので、経済的な負担が小さい。中小領主やその家臣の城は必然的に山城となった。

　安土桃山時代から江戸時代にかけ、広大な領土を統治する大名は、動員できる兵力も数百倍となり、多数の家臣を収容するために広大な面積をもつ平山城や平城を選ばざるをえなくなる。平山城は山を利用して高い石垣を築くことができ、周囲への見通しもきく。そして城下町からは山上にそびえる天守や櫓などがよく見えるため、権威を示すことができる。山城の堅固さと平城の収容能力を併せ持つ理想的な城といえる。平城は政治を行う地に山や丘が見当たらない場合、やむをえず造った城の形態といえる。平地にあるため、自然が守ってくれない分、建造物で防御を固めなくてはいけない。そこで、長大な石垣、多くの櫓や城門、広い堀が必要となる。

Nawabari
(Layout)

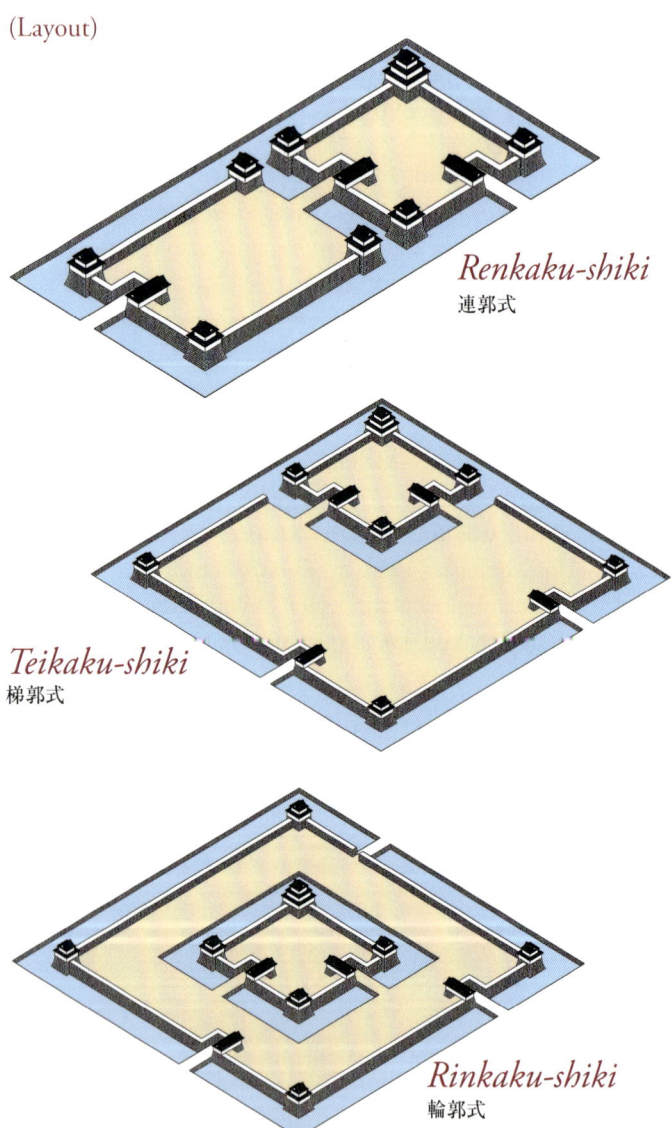

Renkaku-shiki
連郭式

Teikaku-shiki
梯郭式

Rinkaku-shiki
輪郭式

Nawabari (lit. rope stretching) is the basic layout of the castle, the configuration and positioning of its structures. Layouts were determined using lengths of staked ropes to mark out the size and location of the various *kuruwa* (p. 107) or precincts, the length and height of the *ishigaki* (stone walls), the length and depth of the *hori* (moats) and the position of the *tenshu* (tower keep) and *yagura* (turrets).

This planning and positioning of the various *kuruwa* is important for determining the strategic strength of the castle. The three basic castle design layouts are *renkaku-shiki*, *teikaku-shiki* and *rinkaku-shiki*. *Renkaku-shiki* features the "inner" citadel (*honmaru*) and "outer" citadel (*ni-no-maru*) arranged in alignment. The threat to, and the extra defense required on the three exposed sides of the *honmaru* not facing the *ni-no-maru*, is the shortcoming of this layout. The *teikaku-shiki* layout has the *honmaru* surrounded on two or three sides by the *ni-no-maru*. Therefore, the exposed side requires protection by a natural stronghold, such as a river, marsh, or cliffs. *Teikaku-shiki* are best suited to *yamajiro* or *hirayama-jiro* where the natural topography plays a major role in layout. *Rinkaku-shiki* positions the *honmaru* in the center of the *ni-no-maru*, affording the greatest protection on all four sides.

縄張

城の基本設計を縄張という。土木工事にあたって縄を使って長さを測ったことからそう呼ばれるようになったという。縄張とは城を構成する曲輪（p. 107）と呼ばれる区画の大きさや配置、石垣の長さや高さ、堀の幅や深さなどを定め、天守や櫓などの建物の配置を決めることである。

曲輪（郭）の並べ方は城の防御力を決めるため、縄張ではとくに重要である。並べ方は、連郭式、梯郭式、輪郭式の3種類が基本。連郭式は、本丸と二の丸が団子のように一直線に並ぶ。梯郭式は本丸の二方ないし三方を二の丸が取り囲む形式。自然の地形を利用することが多いため、山城や平山城に多い。輪郭式は本丸の四方を二の丸で完全に取り巻いた形式。

Hori and Dorui
(Moats and Earthen Rampart Walls)

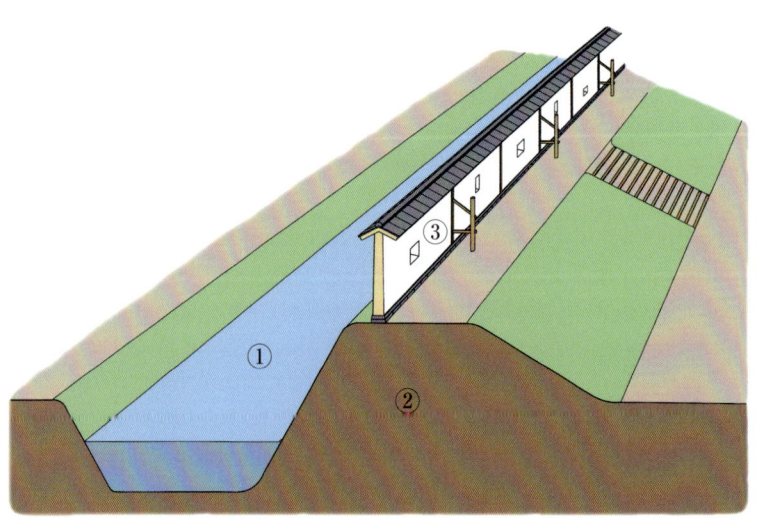

1. *Hori*
2. *Dorui*
3. *Dobei*

①堀　②土塁
③土塀

Drafting: Yuki Kanazawa　作図：金澤雄記

There are two types of moat: *mizubori* (water moats) and *karabori* (dry moats). Being built on mountaintops, it was difficult for medieval *yamajiro* to maintain a reservoir of water and so most *yamajiro* have *karabori* surrounding them, while most castles built on plains make use of water filled trenches called *go* or *mizubori* moats. The average *karabori* is around ten meters wide, and most are a distinctive V shape. *Karabori* cut into ridge-tops to prevent an enemy from advancing further into a mountain-based castle are called *horigiri*, while vertical trenches cut into a mountainside to hinder the lateral movement of enemy troops are called *tatebori*. The wider and deeper the *mizubori*, the greater its defensive capabilities become, as a wider moat lessens the effectiveness of *teppo* (p. 108).

Earthen rampart walls called *dorui* are made mostly from the heaped soil dug from the moats. Almost without exception, medieval castles consisted mainly of such earthworks. Defense-wise, the steep slopes of the compacted soil provided little hand or foot grip, and was therefore considered a more effective defense than stone walls. The downside was that *dorui* were susceptible to weather, particularly in Japan's heavy rainfall conditions.

堀と土塁

　堀は水を湛えた水堀と水のない空堀の2種類がある。中世の山城では、山の上に水を溜めておくことが難しいため堀は空堀で、平地に築かれた近世の城を囲む堀はほとんどが水堀（濠）である。空堀の幅は広くても10m程度で、底をV字形にしたものが多い。尾根筋を分断して尾根上を進んできた敵を防ぐ空堀は堀切という。また山の斜面を縦に切って敵の横方向への移動を防ぐ空堀を竪堀という。水堀は広ければ広いほど防御力が高く、鉄砲（p. 108）の攻撃も防ぐことができる。

　土塁は堀を掘った土を盛って造った城壁で、中世の城はほぼ例外なく土塁だけで造っている。土塁は土を突き固めた急斜面のため、手がかりがなく、防御力は石垣に勝る。ただし雨で傷みやすいのが欠点であった。

The Structure of Ishigaki

1. *Tempa-ishi*
2. *Ai-ishi*
3. *Tsumi-ishi*
4. *Ne-ishi*
5. *Dougi*
6. *Kui*
7. *Uragome*
8. *Kai-ishi*

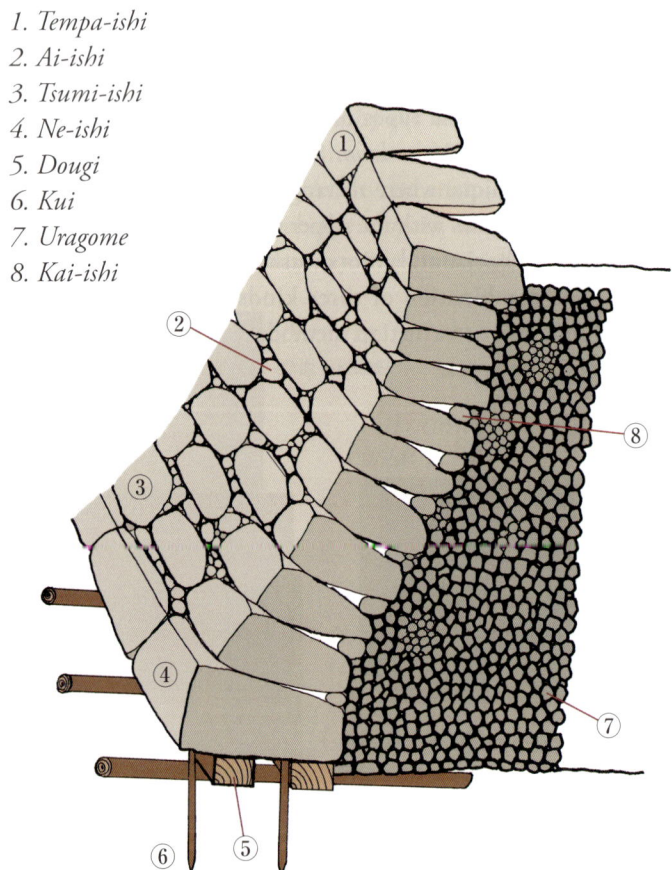

①天端石　②間石　③積み石
④根石　⑤胴木　⑥杭
⑦裏込　⑧飼石

Drafting: Miho Chihara　作図：千原美歩

Foundation work is required before *ishigaki* can be constructed. In the case of *yamajiro* and *hirayama-jiro* where the earth is sufficiently hard, a shallow trench along the base of the wall can be dug, and a *ne-ishi* (foundation stone) can be laid, on which other stones are then piled up on top.

For *hirajiro*, thick pine beams called *dougi* are set horizontally at the bottom of a moat on top of perpendicular pine logs, with *kui*, pine log piles driven into the earth, to fix them in place. *Ne-ishi* are laid atop the *dougi*, and the dry stone walls built up on top of that. *Ishigaki* built without *dougi* are susceptible to collapsing, as the various stones settle at different rates. Use of a *dougi* ensures the sink rate remains stable across the length of the wall, preventing settling problems.

Building stones called *tsumi-ishi* are piled up on the *ne-ishi*, and support each other through contact. The tapered innermost sections of the rocks allow for some leverage in forming the curvature of the walls and are held firmly in place by various-sized rocks called *kai-ishi*. A closely packed filling of smaller stones called *uragome* occupy the space behind the *ne-ishi* and *tsumi-ishi*. These *uragome* serve to support the *ishigaki* and facilitates drainage.

石垣の構造

　石垣の基礎工事は、山城や平山城のように、地上の固い地盤の場合は地面を少し掘って、根石という最下段の石を固定してから積んでいく。

　ところが平城の場合は、地盤が軟弱な水堀の中から石垣を立ち上げるために工夫が必要になる。堀の底に胴木という太い松の角材を敷いて、胴木がずれないように松の丸太の杭を打って固定する。そして、胴木の上に根石を据え、そこから石を積み上げていく。

　根石の上に積み上げていく石を積み石といい、表面より少し奥で互いに接して支え合うが、これを完全に固定するために、さらに後方に飼石（隙間に合った大小の石）を入れる。積み石の背後には裏込という小石をぎっしりと詰める。これは裏から石垣を支え、石垣中の排水を容易にする役割がある。

Curvature and Gradients of Ishigaki

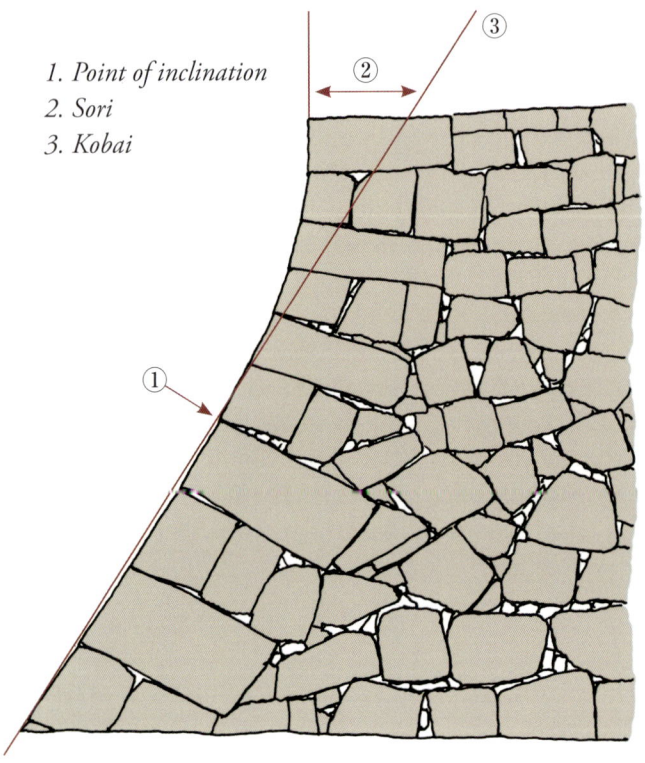

1. *Point of inclination*
2. *Sori*
3. *Kobai*

①反りの始まり
②反り
③勾配

Drafting: Miho Chihara　作図：千原美歩

Japan is an earthquake-prone country, so vertically high *ishigaki* are susceptible to collapsing. For that reason, techniques involving the use of various gradients were devised to permit greater stability and allow higher dry stone wall construction.

The *sori*, the concave pitch of an *ishigaki* with a gentle slope at the lower section gradually becoming steeper, are called *ogi-no-kobai* (lit. folding fan curve), as they resemble the curvature of an opened folding fan. These *ogi-no-kobai* gradients were perfected by the famed warrior and architect of Kumamoto Castle, Kato Kiyomasa (p. 108). Calling it a fan curve leads to the impression that the curvature is a continuous, even shape, however, the lower half of the slope actually rises on a straight angle to the half-way mark before inclining gradually, becoming vertical from about the two-thirds mark. Stone by stone the angle is increased, creating a curve. This upward inflection also prevents the enemy from scaling the walls. For that reason, it is also known as *musha-gaeshi*, or *shinobi-gaeshi* (lit. the warrior, or ninja turn-back).

Not all *ishigaki* are curved. Besides Kato Kiyomasa, another famed castle architect, Todo Takatora (p. 109), built high *ishigaki* with no curvature at all. Instead, he perfected equally efficient, straight edged, yet angled walls.

石垣の反りと勾配

日本は地震多発国であることから、石垣を垂直に高く積むと地震の際に崩れやすい。そこで石垣に緩い勾配をつけて安定させ、高い石垣を築く工夫が生まれた。

石垣の下部は緩い勾配で、上に行くにつれて急勾配になり、最後は垂直にそそり立つ勾配を俗に「扇の勾配」と呼ぶ。扇の勾配は熊本城を築城した加藤清正（p. 108）が好んだため清正流石垣とも呼ばれている。扇の勾配は石垣の半分から3分の2くらいまで直線の勾配で、そこから反りを入れていく。この反りはもちろん石垣を上ってくる敵を阻止するためのものだ。そのため「武者返」「忍返」の名がある。

いっぽう、加藤清正と並ぶ築城の名手であった藤堂高虎（p. 109）はまったく反りのない高い石垣を築いている。一直線に積んだほうが作業的には効率がいい。

Yokoya
(Flank Defense Ports)

1. Byobu-ori   2. Yokoya-gakari

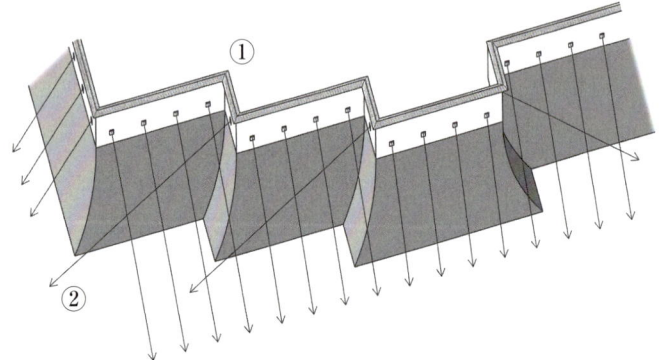

The *ishigaki* and *dorui* of castles often featured protruding, depressed or staggered port sections to increase defense and to allow attack by *yumi* (p. 110) or *teppo* from two directions or more. These sideways defense ports are called *yokoya* (lit. side arrow). One of the castle's most basic defense systems, the function and design of the *yokoya* meant that there was nowhere for the attacking enemy to seek cover.

When designing a castle, the *yokoya* should either extend out beyond the *ishigaki* stone walls or *dorui* earthworks, or be configured as a depression. The corners of a *kuruwa* in particular

---

横矢

城の石垣や土塁の塁線がところどころで折れ曲がっているのは、敵を2方向以上から弓 (p. 110) や鉄砲で攻撃するためである。この側面攻撃を横矢という。敵にとって横矢は防ぎようがないため、城を守るための工夫のなかでも基本中の基本であった。

曲輪の隅部 (角のこと) では、45度の方向が死角になるため、その方向からの敵を攻撃することができない。そこで隅部を内側に折り込めば横矢を仕掛けることができ

are compromised so that 45-degree blind spots prevent the defenders from attacking an invading enemy. This is called an *irisumi* (inset corner). The opposite, an externally protruding corner, is called a *desumi*. For a castle to be effective, the *desumi* must be properly fortified and a defensive *yagura* be constructed. Particularly long sections of wall required centrally located, multiple, or staggered ports for protection (*yokoya-gakari*). These staggered sections are called *byobu-ori*, after the shape of traditional folding screens called *byobu*.

There are various types of *yokoya*. An obtuse angled *yokoya* is called *sumi-otoshi*. Another rare type, where the entire castle wall is of concave construction is known as *hizumi*.

Byobu-ori (Osaka Castle)
屏風折の石垣（大坂城）

る。これを入隅という。また逆に隅部を外側に出っ張らせたものを出隅という。長い城壁では中央部に連続した屈曲部を設けて横矢を掛けるようにした（これを横矢掛という）。その形から屏風折と呼ばれる。

横矢にはさまざまな種類があり、鈍角に屈曲するものは隅落、城壁全体を内側に丸く曲げたものは邪（斜）と呼ぶ。

Kabe and Hei (Walls and Parapets)

The basic castle wall consists of thick layers of piled-up, compacted mud. *Dobei* (lit. mud walls) were fireproof and mostly bulletproof. They are either covered in black-tinted *shitami-itabari* (wooden weather boards) or *nurigome*, a hard covering of *shikkui* (p. 110). Often they take the appearance of *shikkui*-coated walls with the lower sections covered in black, wooden *shitami-ita*. When covered in *shikkui,* the aesthetic appearance is greatly enhanced. With *shitami-ita*, the black is in some cases a coating of high-grade lacquer, but usually a coating of soot and persimmon juice. *Shitami-itabari* provides a rugged, resilient image.

Nurigome (Uwajima Castle)
塗籠（宇和島城）

壁と塀

　城に用いられる壁は土を厚く塗り固めた土壁である（土塀も同じ構造）。土壁を用いたのは防火と防弾のためだ。土壁の仕上げ方法は一般的に塗籠と下見板張の2種類がある。外観は塗籠が白い壁、下見板張が黒い壁である。塗籠は土壁の表面を白漆喰 (p. 110) で仕上げたもので、白く輝く外観はじつに優美。いっぽう下見板張は土壁に黒塗りの板を張ったもの。黒色は高級な漆を用いる場合もあるが、通常は

Shitami-itabari (Matsumoto Castle)
下見板張（松本城）

Nurigome slowly wears thin due to the elements of wind and rain, so re-application every ten years or so is required. *Shitami-ita* protect a mud wall from the elements for around fifty years. Which style to employ depended on the master's aesthetic sense and the cost involved. *Nurigome* requires time and money to maintain, but provides an elegant image, while the *shitami-ita* lacks beauty, but economically is the most sound choice.

煤と柿渋を混ぜてつくった墨を用いる。下見板張は全体として武骨な印象を受ける。
　塗籠は雨に濡れると徐々に漆喰がはがれてしまうため、10年に1度くらい塗りなおさないといけない。壁を風雨から守るために板を張ったのが下見板張であり、50年くらいはもつ。見た目はいいが維持に手間と金がかかる塗籠を選ぶか、見た目は劣るが経済的な下見板張を選ぶかは、築城者の美意識と財力にかかっている。

Sama and Ishi-otoshi
(Loopholes and Stone Dropping Chutes)

The small openings in the walls of castle tower keeps, turrets, and in walls through which to shoot at an enemy with *teppo* or *yumi* while remaining protectively concealed are called *sama*. They are a simple, effective and important mechanism in the defense of the castle.

It is always worth noting the shapes and positions of these loopholes. Long, vertical, rectangular holes set high in a wall are *yazama* or *yumizama* (arrow slits) positioned to suit the height of an archer in a standing position. Holes for guns, *teppo-zama* or *izama*, are set lower in a wall to accommodate a crouching marksman kneeling on one knee for stability.

Another important device alongside the *sama* for protecting the castle is the so-called *ishi-otoshi* (lit. stone dropper). *Ishi-otoshi* was a term mistakenly coined by a tactical researcher in the Edo

Sama (Himeji Castle)　Left: outside　Right: inside
狭間（姫路城　左：外側　右：内側）

狭間と石落

　天守や櫓の壁、土塀に開けられている小さな穴を狭間という。敵に鉄砲や弓を射かけるための穴で、城の守りにおいて重要な仕掛けである。
　注目したいのは狭間の形と位置。縦長の長方形の狭間は矢狭間（弓狭間）で、立って弓を射る姿勢に合わせている。いっぽう鉄砲は片膝をついて構えるため、鉄砲狭間（居狭間）は低い位置にある。

period in an attempt to explain the defensive device along the walls of turrets and keeps jutting out over the edge of the *ishigaki*. The floor of these *ishi-otoshi* can be raised, opening a downward facing window, and so *ishi-otoshi* are thought to have been for the dropping of rocks onto any enemy scaling the walls below. However, the long, narrow openings would limit the size of the stones to be dropped, and the strike rate would be questionable, as no one would climb a wall below such a visible defensive structure. Also, with the curvature of the walls, any stone would not fall far before striking the curved *ishigaki* and bouncing off. The proper term for the opening is *teppo-zama* and its prime use was for the firing of guns on downward angles, providing greater defensive power than the imagined dropping of stones.

Ishi-otoshi (Himeji Castle)
石落（姫路城）

　狭間とともに城を守る重要な仕組みが石落だ。石垣上に建つ天守や櫓の壁から張り出している細長い穴で、石垣を上ってくる敵の上から石を落としたものと考えられていた。しかし、細長い穴から落とす石の大きさも限られるうえ、石は真下にしか落ちないため命中率に疑問が残る。石落は江戸時代の軍学者の想像による名称であり、実際は、下方攻撃用の鉄砲狭間である。

Jomon (Castle Gates)

Mon, or gates, are major defensive elements of a castle. Although there are many types and names of gates, the basic structure and function is the same. Two thick, sturdy main pillars called *kagami-bashira* stand on either side of the gate. A solid connecting beam called *kabuki* lies across the top of the two *kagami-bashira*, to which the inward opening doors are attached. Strengthening and supporting the gate and preventing it from falling are two smaller upright pillars called *hikae-bashira*, which are connected to the rear of the *kagami-bashira* by a stabilizing crossbeam known as a *nuki*.

Yaguramon (Edo Castle's Soto-Sakurada-Mon)
櫓門（江戸城　外桜田門）

城門

　城門の種類や名称はさまざまだが、その基本構造は同じだ。まず城門の正面側に鏡柱という太い主柱を2本立てる。その上に、冠木という太い水平材を渡す。つぎに2本の鏡柱の間に内開きの扉を2枚取り付ける。そして鏡柱の後ろに控柱という柱を立て、鏡柱と控柱を固定するために貫という水平材で連結する。この基本構造の上に載せるものによって城門の種類は変化する。

Koraimon
(Edo Castle's Soto-Sakurada-Mon)

高麗門 (江戸城　外桜田門)

What is then constructed above this basic structure changes the type of gate. The two main differences are single and double-story gates. Two-story castle gates with defensive structures built around the basic gate, such as *yaguramon*, are among a castle's strongest gates. The *yakuimon* and the *koraimon* are representative of the single-story gate variety. *Yakuimon* are castle gates featuring the standard *kagami-bashira* and supporting *hikae-bashira* with a gabled roof across the top, while the *koraimon* features a *kabuki* crossbeam and *nuki* covered in a separate gabled roof.

Despite being of similar design and build, the names of castle gates change according to its location. A castle's main entrance gate is known as the *otemon*, while the rear entrance is known as the *karamete-mon*.

大きく分ければ、上に櫓を載せた櫓門と、平屋建ての門がある。平屋建ての門の代表が薬医門と高麗門だ。薬医門は鏡柱と控柱をまとめてひとつの切妻屋根(本を伏せたような形の屋根)で覆った城門。高麗門は冠木の上に切妻屋根を架け、控柱の上に別の小さな切妻屋根をそれぞれ架けたものである。

　門の名称は、その門が建つ場所の名前で呼ぶのが一般的。城の大手(表口)に建つのが大手門、搦手(裏口)に建つのが搦手門だ。

Masugata (The Death Box)

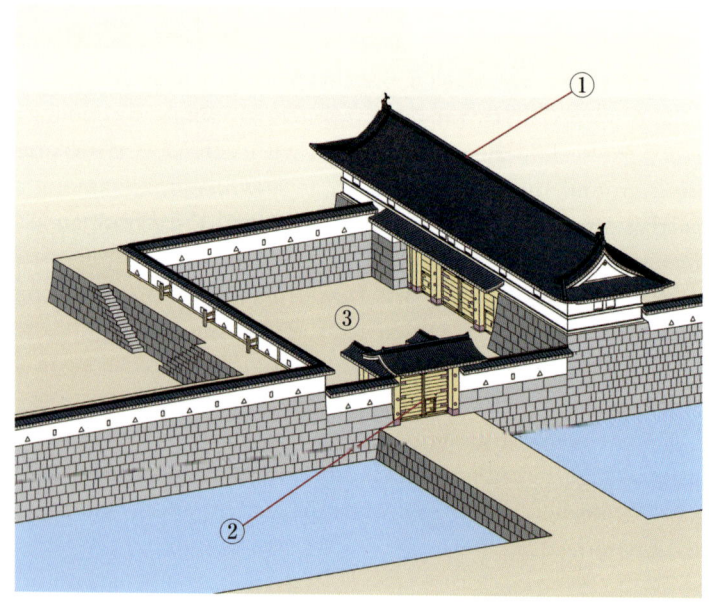

1. *Yaguramon*
2. *Koraimon*
3. *Masugata*

①櫓門
②高麗門
③枡形

Drafting: Yuki Kanazawa　作図：金澤雄記

Entranceways and gates leading to the various *kuruwa* precincts are referred to as *koguchi* (lit. tiger's mouth). The positioning of a *koguchi* is of the utmost importance for defending a castle, and must be protected by a *jomon*. A basic requirement for the design of a strong and effective *koguchi* is that the passage of entry is not straight, but angled, so the enemy cannot see into the *kuruwa* and their momentum is stifled. This also offers multiple defensive points from which to counter attack. Various measures were taken to secure the *koguchi*. The ultimate defense mechanism was the *masugata*, possibly better explained and remembered as a "death box". A *masu* is a wooden box for measuring rice, smaller sizes of which are used for drinking *sake*. The *masugata* gate system is the same box shape. Should the enemy manage to breach the *koraimon*, they would enter a courtyard surrounded by high *ishigaki* or *dorui* walls forming a box shape around them, and with a larger, stronger *yaguramon* at right angles to their entry point. Defensive fire from guns or arrows could then be directed down from all angles at the attacking enemy now trapped in the courtyard. These two gates are called *masugata-mon*.

ますがた
枡形

　曲輪の入口を虎口といい、縄張ではもっとも重要なポイントとなる。通常は、虎口に城門を建てる。虎口を堅固にするための基本は、通路を折り曲げること。通路を曲げれば、虎口から曲輪内を見通すことができないので、敵の勢いを削ぐことができる。なによりも通路を曲げることの目的は敵に横矢を掛けることである。虎口を厳重にするためにさまざまな工夫がこらされたが、その究極形が枡形である。枡とは米を量る方形の容器のことで、虎口の枡形は枡の形をした四角形の小さな広場のことだ。石垣や土塁で四角形の広場を設け、外側の入口に高麗門、内側の入口に櫓門を建てる。この2つの門を合わせて枡形門と呼ぶ。外側の高麗門を突破して枡形に入った敵は、周囲の城壁上から側面と背面を攻撃され、正面の櫓門からも射撃される。

Yagura (Turrets)

Hira-Yagura
(Himeji Castle Taiko-Yagura)

平櫓（姫路城太鼓櫓）

Niju-Yagura
(Nijo Castle Tonan-Sumi-Yagura)

二重櫓（二条城東南隅櫓）

Sanju-Yagura
(Nagoya Castle Seihoku-Sumi-Yagura)

三重櫓（名古屋城西北隅櫓）

Yagura are defensive turrets and storerooms often found atop *ishigaki* corners and strategic positions around the castle allowing covering fire to adjacent walls. *Yagura* (lit. arrow storehouse) served as storerooms for armor, weapons and provisions, and for defense in wartime. Originally elevated watchtowers, the tower-like turrets known as *yagura* today first appeared in the early to mid 16th century, and predate the *tenshu* tower keep. An integral part of a castle's defense, *yagura* built on the corners of *kuruwa* are called *sumi-yagura*. *Yagura* are classified by the number of visible outward roofs. *Hira-yagura,* or *ichiju-yagura,* are single-floored turrets. *Niju-yagura*, the most basic and widely built *yagura*, had two roofs, while *sanju-yagura* sported three. A *sanju-yagura* was often substituted for a keep in a castle too small to be allowed a *tenshu*.

Hira-yagura were rarely used as a *sumi-yagura* as they were too low to provide watchtower view capabilities. Instead, *tsuke-yagura* and *tsuzuki-yagura* were often built as attachments to *tenshu* and *sanju-yagura*. Corridor-like *hira-yagura,* built along the upper ramparts around the *honmaru* and important gates, were referred to as *tamon-yagura*, and took on defensive capabilities in times of attack by permitting arrow and gunfire from the many windows along their length.

櫓

櫓（矢倉）は平時は倉庫であり、戦時には攻撃の拠点であった。近世城郭の櫓は、天守に先立って16世紀中期に出現した。城の防備で重要な箇所は曲輪の隅部であることから、櫓は曲輪の隅に建てられることが多い。ゆえに一般に櫓は隅櫓とも呼ばれる。櫓は外観の屋根の数によって、平櫓（一重）、二重櫓、三重櫓に分類され、三重櫓は最高の格式の櫓で、天守をもたない城では天守の代用とされた。二重櫓は櫓の基本形であり、もっとも多く造られた。

平櫓は物見の効果が少ないため隅櫓として建てられることは少なく、天守や三重櫓に付属した付櫓（続櫓）として建てられることが多かった。また、城壁の上に長く続く平櫓を多門櫓と呼ぶ。多門櫓は本丸の周囲や重要な城門の付近に建てられ、有事の際には鉄壁の防御力を発揮した。

The Many Names of Yagura

Tsukimi-Yagura (Okayama Castle)
月見櫓（岡山城）

Fushimi-Yagura (Fukuyama Castle)
伏見櫓（福山城）

Early-modern castles often had a large number of *yagura* turrets built around the castle's perimeter. The many different names of the *yagura* indicate their role. *Yagura* stored weapons or armor in peacetime. *Teppo-yagura* stored matchlock guns, *yumi-yagura* housed bows, the *ensho-yagura* kept gunpowder, military provisions and emergency rations were placed in the *hoshi-ii-yagura,* and the *shio-yagura* was for keeping salt. The *taiko-yagura*, or drum tower, contained a large drum used for time keeping and communications. Large window spaces allowed the sound to reverberate for some distance. The *shiomi-yagura* was for watching the ocean. The *tsukimi-yagura* allowed the castle lord to enjoy moon viewing parties. The lady of the castle may have had a *kesho-yagura* in which to apply her make-up. Edo Castle's *fujimi-yagura* was so named as one could see Mt. Fuji from the turret, while some *yagura* received their names from the castles they formerly served, such as Fukuyama Castle's *fushimi-yagura* which was originally part of Fushimi Castle before being dismantled and rebuilt at Fukuyama Castle.

櫓の名称

　近世城郭では数多くの櫓を建て並べていた。櫓の名称はその役割を示したものが多い。平時に武器や武具を貯蔵していた櫓は、鉄砲櫓、弓櫓、煙硝櫓の名があり、兵糧を蓄えていた櫓は干飯櫓、塩櫓などと呼ばれた。特殊な用途としては時間を知らせるための太鼓を置いた太鼓櫓があり、音を遠くまで響かせるために窓を大きく開けている。そのほか潮見櫓は海上を監視するため、月見櫓は城主が月見を楽しむため、化粧櫓は城主夫人など身分の高い女性が化粧をするためで、江戸城の富士見櫓は富士を眺望できたのが名の由来。また、移築された櫓はかつての城名で呼ばれることがある。福山城の伏見櫓（旧伏見城の櫓）がその代表だ。

Tenshu (Tower Keeps)

Boro-gata Tenshu (Matsue Castle)
望楼型天守（松江城）

Soto-gata Tenshu (Uwajima Castle)
層塔型天守（宇和島城）

The *tenshu* is the central tower-like building symbolizing the prestige and authority of the castle's lord. In the late Muromachi period, large towering *yagura* of three and four stories began to appear in central western Japan, however the first to construct a luxurious high-rise tower keep and call it a *tenshu* was Oda Nobunaga (p. 111). Nobunaga's magnificent Azuchi Castle was an innovation in castle architecture. In general, castles made after Azuchi's *tenshu* are considered *kinsei-jokaku*, or early modern castles.

Tenshu are divided into two types—*boro-gata* and *soto-gata*—and are defined by their shape and construction. *Boro-gata* have a single or two-story base building with *irimoya-zukuri* hip-and-gable styled roof (p. 112) with a two or three-story watchtower built on top. The advantage of the *boro-gata* type *tenshu* was that even if the *tenshu*'s stone base was of uneven shape, such as trapezoid, or even pentagonal due to the lay of the land, a *tenshu* could still be constructed. This was beneficial during wartime, as time was not wasted on squaring up the base, and a strong fortress could be quickly established. *Soto-gata tenshu* are simpler to build, and like multi-story temple pagodas, have roofing separating each ascending, smaller tiered level like a wedding cake.

天守

　天守は城の中心となる建物で、城主の権威を象徴するものだ。室町時代末期、近畿には3階や4階建ての大型の櫓が出現していたが、それを豪華な高層建築に変えて「天主」(のちに一般には天守)と名付けたのが、安土城を築いた織田信長 (p. 111) である。天守が出現した安土城以降の城を「近世城郭」と呼ぶ。

　天守の形式は屋根の構造から望楼型と層塔型の2種に分けられる。望楼型は一重または二重の入母屋造 (p. 112) 建物を基部として、その上に二重または三重の別の建物を載せた形式である。一方、層塔型は寺院の五重塔や三重塔のように、各重の屋根を四方に葺き下ろした形式である。望楼型は天守台 (天守を建てる石垣) の平面がゆがんでいても建てられる利点があり、層塔型は構造が単純なので工期を短縮できる利点があった。

Inside the Tenshu

Azuchi Castle *Tenshu*
(Recreated sectional view)

安土城天主 復元断面図

Himeji Castle *Tenshu*
(Inside)

姫路城天守内部

Only Oda Nobunaga lived in his castle's *tenshu*. It was luxurious, built in the samurai-preferred *shoin-zukuri* (p. 112) style of residential architecture. Its inner walls were adorned with paintings by leading contemporary artists. Toyotomi Hideyoshi (p. 113) made his gorgeous *tenshu* at Osaka Castle and proudly gave tours of the opulent interiors to his guests. Hideyoshi lived not in the keep, but in the *honmaru* palace.

Unlike Nobunaga and Hideyoshi, Tokugawa Ieyasu (p. 114), founder of the Edo Shogunate, was known to be very frugal and would not allow people inside of his *tenshu* as there was nothing to see. Except for toilets and a large sink for washing food in Himeji Castle, none of the few remaining original *tenshu* show any examples of luxury. Instead, the emphasis is on functionality in times of *rojo* (p. 115). One rare example of comfort was *tatami* (p. 115) mats on most of the *tenshu* floors for samurai to sleep on. During the Edo period, the lord of the castle would rarely enter the *tenshu*, as it was seen as the last refuge in times of war, and so it was deemed unlucky for the lord to enter the *tenshu* during peacetime.

天守の内部

　天守に住んだ城主は歴史上で織田信長ひとりである。信長が築いた安土城天主の内部は豪華な書院造 (p. 112) で、当代随一の絵師による障壁画で彩られていた。豊臣秀吉 (p. 113) も居城の大坂城の天守内部を豪華に造ったが、秀吉が客人を案内して自慢するための見学施設と化し、秀吉自身は本丸御殿に住んだ。

　そののち、江戸幕府を開いた徳川家康 (p. 114) になると天守内部は質素になり、天守には人もあげなくなってしまう。城主が天守に入ることすらめったになくなり、現存の天守では豪華な内部をもったものはひとつもなく、有事の際に籠城 (p. 115) するための機能を重視したものになっている。姫路城天守の内部には食材を洗うための大きな流しが設置され、便所も設けられている。また、有事の際に兵が寝泊まりするために、天守の内部には畳 (p. 115) が敷きつめられていた。

Goten (Palaces)

Kuro-Shoin (Nijo Castle)
黒書院（二条城）

Ni-no-Maru Goten (Kakegawa Castle)
掛川城二の丸御殿

The *goten* (palace) served as both the residence of the lord and his family, as well as the regional government office. Early *yamajiro* usually had the palace located some distance away, often below the mountain on which the castle was built. In comparison, later *hirayama-jiro* and *hirajiro* featured the *goten* on flat land within the castle confines.

Goten required large areas of land. They were usually configured into private residence and areas for official duties called *omote*, with the lords' audience chambers, meeting rooms and domain administrative offices. The *omote goten*, *hiroma* and *shoin* rooms were primarily audience chambers and official rooms of the finest architecture, decorated with the most gorgeous wall paintings. The lord's official living quarters included *furo* (p. 116), *chashitsu* (p. 116), rest and entertainment facilities, and even a *Noh* stage (p. 117) in some cases. The *oku* was a private area for the lord's immediate family that was off limits to men besides the lord himself and was the domain of the maids and womenfolk, for whom the *naga-tsubone* (lit. long corridor) dormitories were built.

御殿

　御殿は政庁を兼ねた城主の住居である。中世の城の大部分は山の上に築かれ（山城）、城主の御殿（居館）は山城から少し離れた平地や山城の麓に造られた。いっぽう、近世の平山城や平城では城内の平地に御殿が建てられるのが特徴である。
　御殿の構成は、対面の儀式と藩政を行うための「表」と城主の私邸である「奥」に分かれる。表の代表的な殿舎は対面の場である表御殿で、一般的に玄関・広間・書院からなる。なかでも広間と書院は贅を尽くした最高級の建築で、豪華な障壁画で飾られた。さらに役所や台所があり、城主の公邸である中奥には風呂 (p. 116)、茶室 (p. 116)、能舞台 (p. 117) など休息・娯楽施設も付属していた。奥は城主の私的空間で、表の役人は立ち入ることができず、すべては御殿女中と呼ばれる女性たちが仕切っていた。そのため、奥には女中たちが暮らす長局が建てられた。

Tei-en (Gardens)

Muromachi period aristocratic *daimyo* desired the culture of the capital and imitated the opulent lifestyle and mansions of the shogun by having elegant gardens created as part of their living quarters. Among the best remaining examples are the Asakura mansion gardens of Ichijodani (Fukui prefecture) and the Ouchi clan mansion gardens (Yamaguchi prefecture). Another of the early modern castles to feature an impressive garden was Toyotomi Hideyoshi's Osaka Castle. An area modeled after the rural countryside, known as the Yamazato Kuruwa, contained a palace for tea ceremonies and banquets.

While the central *honmaru* gardens were enjoyable, often larger, more impressive gardens would be established in a wider area a short distance from the castle's central bailey. These *daimyo* gardens featured large ponds or lakes surrounded by a landscape of rocks and hills representing natural settings, and paths allowing one to stroll at leisure. Such gardens were used to entertain the lord's guests with outdoor tea ceremonies or moon viewing parties, and were open to his retainers as a place of relaxation.

庭園

　室町時代の守護大名は京の文化に憧れ、将軍の邸宅である「花の御所」をまねて、居館に庭園を営んだ。一乗谷朝倉館（福井県）や大内氏館（山口県）がその例だ。近世城郭ではじめて城内に庭園を営んだのは豊臣秀吉の大坂城といわれる。「山里曲輪」という田園を模した広大な庭園で、御殿や茶室を建て、茶会や宴会が催された。
　それ以降、近世の城では御殿と庭園はセットとなり、本丸御殿と庭園というように、城内の御殿に付属したものもあれば、城の中心からやや離れた平地に広大な外園を営むこともあった。大名庭園の多くは広い池があり、その周囲に山や丘を模した起伏をつくって大きな石を配置したもので、池の周囲を散策できる回遊式庭園と呼ばれる様式だ。この庭園で城主は茶会や月見を楽しんだり、客人をもてなしたりした。

Joka-machi (Castle Towns)

Joka-machi were residential and economic centers and an important line of defense in times of attack. For that reason, the *joka-machi's* design was just as important as that of the castle itself. The *kaido* (p. 117) and streets of the *joka-machi* would curve or bend intentionally and cul-de-sacs were created to confuse and halt attacking enemy.

Samurai residences were grouped close to the castle in the *samurai-machi*, while a larger segment of the town was occupied by merchants, tradespeople and craftsmen. The townsfolk usually lived in areas named after their occupation, skill or art, for example, kimono and clothing traders lived in *gofuku-machi* (clothing district), blacksmiths in *kaji-machi* (blacksmith district), paper merchants were found in *kamiya-machi* (papershop district), and so on. The division between *samurai-machi* and that of the townsfolk was clearly delineated. Property taxes were based on the width of the property frontage, so the townsfolk built narrow, street-facing *machiya* townhouses.

The strategically positioned *tera-machi* (Buddhist temple district) served as a fine defense against attacks. Temples were surrounded by tall *dobei* walls which could act as a barrier against invading forces. The large, raised main prayer hall located in the middle could be used as a military base in times of emergency.

城下町

　城を取り巻く城下町は経済的中心であるとともに、有事の際には重要な防御線となる。城下町の街道 (p. 117) や街路は、敵が侵入した際の市街戦を想定して意図的に曲げたり、袋小路にしたりすることもあった。

　城下町は、侍屋敷が集まる侍町、商工業を営む町人たちが住む町家（町屋）が集まる町人地が大部分を占める。侍町と町人地は明確に区画分けされた。町家は街路に面して建つのが原則で、街路に面した間口が狭く、それに対して奥行きが長い。町人地の町名は、呉服町、鍛冶町、紙屋町など、商工業者の職業に関係してつけられることも多かった。

　城下町では寺院を集めることも多く、その区画を寺町と呼ぶ。寺院は石垣や土塀で取り巻かれ、有事の際の軍事拠点としての役割を与えられていた。

Samurai-yashiki (Samurai Residences)

Saigo Family *Nagayamon* (Hikone City)
西郷家長屋門（彦根市）

Mekata Family Main Residence (Iwakuni City)

目加田家主屋（岩国市）

Samurai lived and worked in castles. Samurai homes were generally single-story structures called *samurai-yashiki*. These were grouped together near the castle, forming a *samurai-machi* (samurai town) with each family located in a suitable district and residence according to each vassals' appointed position or job title, status, and income. Simply put, the higher ranked you were, the closer to the castle center and the larger your allocated land. Along the front of senior and intermediate samurai properties was a large, long building consisting of a gate. This was called a *nagayamon*. Samurai below intermediate rank could not have *nagayamon*, and made do with gates of various size and style, depending upon their status and income. Similarly, the properties were surrounded by *dobei* walls or even hedges depending on status and income.

Senior retainers' homes were designed similar to those of the castle lord, with official reception areas at the front and separate living quarters in the back. The partitioning of the reception room and the living room became the archetype of Japanese-style housing from the Meiji period.

侍屋敷

　城には多くの武士が勤務するため、その住居が必要である。これを侍屋敷という。侍屋敷が並ぶ区画が侍町で、家臣の役職や石高に応じて敷地が貸し与えられ、身分相応の屋敷が建てられた。上級や中級の家臣は、屋敷の正面に長大な長屋を建ててその一部に門を設けた。これを長屋門という。長屋門を建てることができない中級以下の家臣の屋敷では、土塀や生垣で囲んで簡略な表門を建てた。

　侍屋敷は基本的に平屋建てで、上級の家臣の屋敷は城主の御殿と同じように、表（接客空間）と奥（生活空間）が別棟になっていたが、中級以下の家臣の屋敷は1棟の主屋のなかで、表と奥を分けた。この客間と居間を区分することが、明治以降の和風住宅の原型になっている。

Chapter 2

History of Castles

第二章

城の歴史

Yayoi−Heian Periods

Japan's castles began as *kango-shuraku* (moat-surrounded villages) in the Iron Age Yayoi period (300 BC-300 AD). The accumulation of wealth in an agrarian society created a need to protect and defend the village, hence fortifications developed. Settlements were made on hills overlooking the important rice fields with trenches or moats and simple earthworks surrounding the colony.

The Nara period (710-794) and Heian period (794-1185) capitals, Heijokyo and Heiankyo, were not enclosed by high walls like Chinese cities, as foreign attack was not a concern. However, conflict between the native Ezo (Emishi) peoples of north-eastern Japan led to the construction of a large fortified administrative settlement called Taga Castle (Miyagi prefecture), a fine example of an early fortification.

弥生時代〜平安時代

日本の城は、弥生時代の環濠集落に始まる。農耕社会は富の蓄積をもたらし、富の争奪が起こる。その結果、集落を防備する必要が生まれた。そこで集落は水田を見下ろす高台に設け、集落の周囲に堀や土塁をめぐらせた。これを環濠集落という。

奈良時代と平安時代の都である平城京や平安京は、対外的危機が迫っていなかったため中国の城郭都市のような高い城壁で都を囲わなかった。いっぽうで、東北では蝦夷と呼ばれる民と中央政権との抗争があり、多賀城（宮城県）など、防御施設をともなう政庁が設置された。

Kamakura–Early Muromachi Periods

By the Medieval Ages, privately built fortifications began to appear. The warlords who built these small fortresses were governors of limited territories with little economic strength and an army of only a few dozen warriors.

From the 14th to the 15th century, the majority of castles were *yamajiro*, where mountain summits and ridges were shaved and leveled to make space for *kuruwa*.

Yamajiro of this era were places of refuge in times of attack. Living in the castle at the top of a mountain was considered inconvenient, and so the lord usually lived and worked in a *kyokan* (manor residence) built on level ground at the base of the mountain or a short distance away. These *kyokan* were protected by defensive structures and encircled by both *dorui* and *hori*, and as such could be recognized in a broad sense as a castle. This combination of *kyokan* peacetime living quarters and mountaintop *yamajiro* for wartime use were referred to as *chusei-jokan* (lit. medieval castle houses).

鎌倉時代〜室町時代前期

　中世に武士が登場すると私的な築城が行われるようになる。彼らの経済力は低く、その造る城もせいぜい数十人が守備するような小規模なものだった。14〜15世紀にかけての城の大多数は山頂部や尾根筋を削平して曲輪（郭）を造った山城で、有事の際に逃げ込むための城であった。

　山城は生活に不便なため、城主はふだん城下の居館に住んでいた。居館は周囲に土塁や堀などをめぐらした武装化した住居で、これも広い意味では城に含まれる。今日では山城と居館を合わせて「中世城館」と呼んでいる。

Late Muromachi Period

By the late Muromachi period (or Sengoku period, 1336-1573) with neighboring warlords brought under their control by either choice or by force, the larger, militarily and financially more powerful *daimyo* class of warlords called *sengoku-daimyo* began to emerge. The greater numbers of troops allowing for mass mobilization and greater economic strength led to large-scale castle construction.

The majority of *chusei-jokaku* (medieval castles) remained *yamajiro* during the Sengoku period. Relatively high and large mountains were chosen for these, and large numbers of *kuruwa*, over 100 in some cases, were carved from the mountain. Effective defensive features were developed making use of the natural terrain and additional large-scale earthworks, such as the digging of a dry moat, were carried out. As civil wars across Japan intensified, the *kyokan* at the base of the castle came under greater threat, and the lord's living quarters began to be relocated within the safer, central baileys of the *yamajiro*. Among these large-scale medieval castles, the Mori clan's Yoshida Koriyama Castle (Hiroshima prefecture) and the Uesugi clan's Kasugayama Castle (Niigata prefecture) are seen as typical examples.

The ruins of Takeda Shingen's (1521-73) *kyokan* can be found in Kofu City, Yamanashi prefecture, where the Takeda Shrine now

室町時代後期（戦国時代）

室町時代後期（戦国時代）になると、近隣の領主を配下に従えて強大化した領主の戦国大名が現れる。動員できる兵の数が飛躍的に増して、経済力も豊かになると、それにともなって大規模な城が造られるようになった。

戦国時代の「中世城郭」の大多数は山城である。立地は比高の大きな山が選ばれ、曲輪の数が100を超えるような大規模な城が造られた。防御施設は地形を巧みに造成して、大規模な土塁を築いたり、深い空堀を掘ったりするようになる。さらに

①尾根　②堀切　③物見台
④本丸　⑤二の丸　⑥出の丸
⑦土塁（切岸）　⑧堅堀

1. O-ne　*2. Horigiri*
3. Monomidai
4. Honmaru
5. Ni-no-maru
6. De-no-maru
7. Dorui (Kirigishi)
8. Tatebori

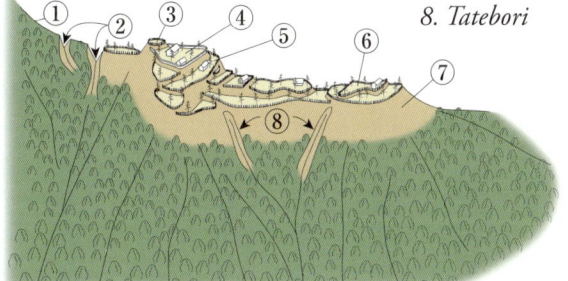

Medieval *Yamajiro* (Yoshida Koriyama Castle)
中世の山城（吉田郡山城）

stands. Many Sengoku warlords built *kyokan* within the confines of their *yamajiro*, however Shingen did not build a large *yamajiro*, and instead spent his days of peace within the Tsutsujigasaki Palace, a superb residence located on a plain. Should he ever come under the threat of attacks, he could withdraw to nearby Yogaiyama Castle, the remains of which extend 280m east to west, and about 190m north to south, and are surrounded by well-kept *mizubori*, *karabori*, and *dorui* protecting the *kuruwa*, allowing us to determine the form of the Sengoku period *kyokan*.

　戦乱が恒常化するにともない、それまで平地にあった城主の居館が山城の内に収容されるようになる。このような大規模な中世城郭としては、毛利氏の吉田郡山城（広島県）や上杉氏の春日山城（新潟県）などが代表としてあげられる。
　多くの戦国大名が山城の内に居館を設けるなかで、武田信玄（1521〜73）は、山城の大城郭を築かず、平時は平地の居館である躑躅ヶ崎館（現在は武田神社）で暮らした。有事の際の備えとしては、近くに詰の城である要害山城を設けていた。

In particular, the *dorui* surrounding the innermost precinct reached heights of 9m, and were more than 21m wide at their base.

Shingen did engage in castle construction, and he was highly skilled at designing combat-ready fortresses. He was most aggressive in invading neighboring provinces, and in doing so, established many frontline castles. The Takeda castles often featured *umadashi*, barbican-like protective barriers consisting of *dorui* earthworks and *karabori*, creating a small compound blocking direct access to the *koguchi*. This *umadashi* defended the entranceway from enemy attack and provided cover for the defending samurai departing and entering the castle. This castle defense technology was later adopted by the Tokugawa for use in their castles too.

Tsutsujigasaki Yakata
(Takeda Shrine)

躑躅ヶ崎館（武田神社）
©ジョー/PIXTA（ピクスタ）

躑躅ヶ崎館跡は東西約280m、南北約190mの敷地に、曲輪、土塁、水堀、空堀などの遺構をよくとどめ、戦国時代の居館の姿を知ることができる。とくに主郭の土塁は高さ9m、基底部の幅が21mを超える大規模なものだ。

信玄は城を造らなかったわけではない。近隣諸国への積極的な侵攻を行い、その最前線に多くの城を築いている。武田氏が築いた城は、馬出（虎口前面を遮断する土塁と空堀）に見られるように、守りは固く、かつ出撃しやすい構造をしており、実戦用の城をつくるのが上手だった。武田氏滅亡後、この築城技術は徳川家康に受け継がれて、徳川氏の城づくりに生かされた。

Castles of the Rulers

The Sengoku, or Warring States period, saw violent battles rage across Japan, and so castle expansion and development increased. Oda Nobunaga, in his efforts to unify the nation took the art of castle construction to the next level with his most innovative and magnificent residence and military stronghold, Azuchi Castle. Nobunaga made extensive use of *ishigaki* around the castle's central areas and at the base of the towering *tenshu* and palace. Azuchi Castle inspired the following wave of large-scale early modern castles.

Nobunaga's successor, Toyotomi Hideyoshi had the equally impressive Osaka Castle completed by a system assigning various *daimyo* construction tasks without compensation, known as *Tenkabushin*. Following Hideyoshi's unification, castle construction spread. This *Tenkabushin* process was adopted by Tokugawa Ieyasu when enlarging Edo Castle and building his son's residence and stronghold, Nagoya Castle, amongst others. Nobunaga, Hideyoshi and Ieyasu built huge castles with magnificent *tenshu* to show their financial and military authority.

天下人の城

戦国時代の戦乱に対応して、城は拡張、強化されていった。発展した築城技術を集大成して居城の安土城を築いたのが、天下統一事業の頂点に立った織田信長である。安土城は城の中心部に石垣を多用し、天主をあげ、城内に御殿を建てたもので、この城をもって本格的な「近世城郭」が誕生したといえる。

信長の後継者となった豊臣秀吉は、諸大名に無償で工事を割り当てる「天下普請(てんかぶしん)」によって大坂城を完成。近世城郭は秀吉の天下統一にともなって全国に普及する。天下普請は徳川家康によって引き継がれ、居城の江戸城、家康の子の居城である名古屋城などが天下普請によって築かれていった。信長、秀吉、家康という天下人が築いた巨城と壮麗な天守は、天下にその権威を知らしめるためのものだった。

Azuchi Castle
(Omi Hachiman, Shiga)

Tenshu of Azuchi Castle
安土城天主 復元図

Azuchi Castle was a splendid castle built on Mt. Azuchi on the eastern banks of Lake Biwa from 1576. The castle featured extensive use of *ishigaki* surrounding the uppermost *honmaru* precincts, and at the summit, the first-ever five-level *tenshu* tower keep. Surrounding this imposing keep was the grandest of *goten* palaces.

The tower keep was constructed atop an unequal-sided octagonal, stone-lined base with the first floor built to match this shape. The tower was a high-rise of its time, an impressive 33m from the base to the roof ridge and containing six floors, an underground basement storage area, and five stories soaring above. It was the equivalent height of a modern-day ten-floor building. The first to the third floors were the finest examples of *shoin-zukuri,* aristocratic mansion architecture, characterized by a symmetrical arrangement of chambers around a central main superstructure. The walls, doors and partitions were covered in gold leaf and decorated by elegant paintings by the leading artists of the day.

Azuchi Castle was destroyed in a fire three years after completion following the assassination of its master, Oda Nobunaga in 1582.

安土城（滋賀県近江八幡市）

　安土城は琵琶湖の東岸に位置する安土山に築かれた城である。天正4年（1576）に築城を開始。山頂に石垣造りの本丸を置き、天主台の上に史上初の五重の天主をあげた。さらに天主の周囲には豪壮な御殿を建て並べていた。

　天主台は山頂部分を造成した不等辺八角形で、1階も天主台に合わせて不等辺八角形をしていたと考えられている。内部は地上6階、地下1階で、高さは天主地階から五重目の棟木まで約33mあった。現在の10階建てのビルに相当し、当時としては超高層建築といえる。1階から3階までは最高級の書院造の建物を積み重ねたような構造で、建具や壁には当代一流の絵師による金碧障壁画が描かれた。

　安土城は完成からわずか3年、天正10年（1582）に織田信長の死とともに焼失した。

Osaka Castle
(Chuo, Osaka)

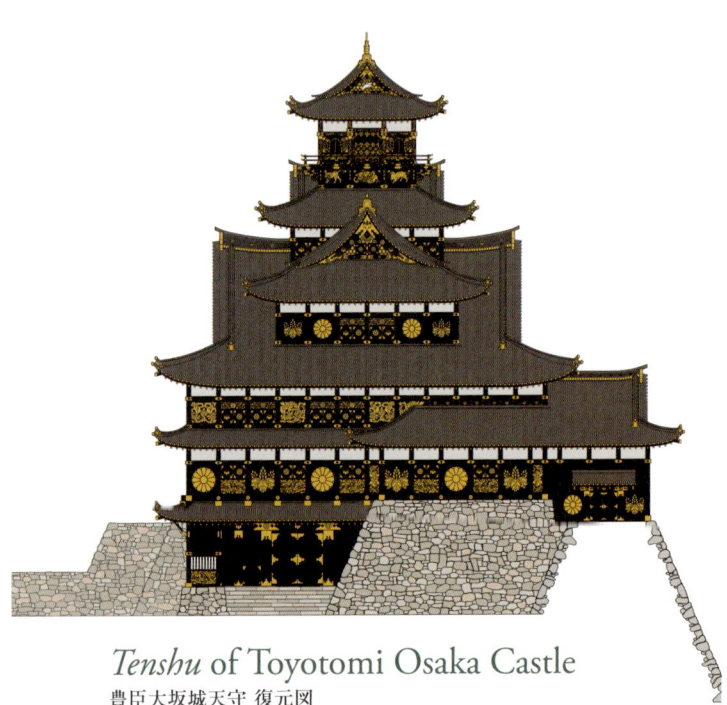

Tenshu of Toyotomi Osaka Castle
豊臣大坂城天守 復元図

Osaka Castle was constructed atop the ruins of the Ishiyama Hongan-ji, a True Prue Land Buddist temple. Toyotomi Hideyoshi succeeded Oda Nobunaga in 1583, and two years later had completed construction of a five-story keep at the center of Osaka.

The tower was similar to that of Azuchi Castle, in that it was a *boro-gata* construction featuring six floors with two underground basements. The scale of the *tenshu* was on a par with Azuchi Castle, however the exterior was lacquered black and decorated with large peony flowers in an arabesque pattern rendered in gold along with *kirimon*, *kikumon* and *tomoemon* crests. Gold was used lavishly on the exterior so much so it surpassed the grandeur of Azuchi Castle. The *shachi-gawara* (or *shachihoko*), the roof top decorative devices with the head of a dragon and the body of a scaly fish, and other decorative roofing tiles, such as *nokimaru-gawara*, the rounded eve edge tiles, and *nokihira-gawara*, the rectangular eve edge tiles were all finished in gold.

Hideyoshi was more than eager to conduct invited guests on tours of the luxurious *tenshu* interiors, as it served to enhance his reputation, power and authority. Once the *tenshu* was completed, work continued on the rest of the castle until Hideyoshi's death

大坂城（大阪市中央区）

　大坂城が建つ地は、もとは浄土真宗の本山・石山本願寺の跡地である。織田信長の跡を継いだ羽柴（のちの豊臣）秀吉は天正11年（1583）に大坂城の築城を開始し、2年後の天正13年頃には五重の天守が完成した。

　天守は外観五重、内部は6階、地下2階で、安土城を継承する望楼型の天守だった。天守の規模は安土城と大きく変わらないが、外観の壁面を黒漆塗りにし、そこに金色に輝く大きな牡丹唐草、桐紋、菊紋、巴紋などの彫刻をぎっしりと嵌め込んでいた。また、鯱瓦（鯱／頭は龍、体は魚の想像上の霊魚をかたどった瓦）、飾り瓦、軒丸瓦（軒先の屋根の縁端を飾る丸瓦）、軒平瓦（同仕様の平瓦）などにも黄金をふんだんに用いており、外観の豪華さでは安土城を完全に凌駕していた。

in 1598, when the *san-no-maru* and entire castle's outermost perimeter moat was finally completed. The total construction including *dorui*, *mizubori* and *karabori*, covered an area of around 4km^2.

Hideyoshi's death allowed Tokugawa Ieyasu to seize control of the nation in the decisive Battle of Sekigahara in 1600. Many samurai remained loyal to the Toyotomi clan, and so in 1614, in an effort to completely destroy any potential opposition, Ieyasu ordered 190,000 samurai to lay siege to Osaka Castle, with Hideyoshi's son and heir, Hideyori (1593-1615) and some 90,000 *ronin* (masterless samurai) inside. This winter siege of Osaka ended with the Tokugawa forces filling in moats and leveling the outer defenses up to the *ni-no-maru*. The following summer, 1615, the Tokugawa forces regrouped and attacked Osaka Castle yet again.

Osaka Castle was destroyed and later completely rebuilt by the Tokugawa through the *Tenkabushin* system in order to monitor and control the western region *daimyo*. Under the advice of Todo Takatora, the moats were re-dug wider and the *ishigaki* built much higher—up to 30 meters in places—and the *tenshu* was

秀吉は客人を招いては豪華な天守内部を好んで案内した。天下人の権威を知らしめるためである。天守が完成したのちも城の拡張工事は続けられ、秀吉が死ぬ慶長3年（1598）までに、三の丸や城全体を囲む総構などが完成した。総構は水堀（一部空堀）と土塁で構築され、約2km四方の規模を誇った。

秀吉の死後、慶長5年（1600）の関ヶ原の戦いで天下の主導権を握った徳川家康は、秀吉の遺児の秀頼（1593～1615）を潰すために挑発を繰り返し、ついに慶長19年（1614）の冬、大坂城を19万の兵で囲んだ（大坂冬の陣）。このとき大坂城には諸国の浪人を含めた9万人が籠城し、徳川方の兵を総構で完全に防ぎ切った。講和ののち、徳川方は講和条件を無視して二の丸までを完全に破壊し、大坂城は本丸

repositioned. The new white plastered *tenshu* was 1.5 times bigger than the Toyotomi *tenshu* and featured a *sanju-yagura* alongside. Both have long since burned down.

The current concrete replica, built in 1931, was supposed to resemble the Toyotomi *tenshu*, but sits atop the Tokugawa base.

を残して平地になってしまう。そして翌年 (1615) の夏にふたたび大坂城は徳川方に攻められ、あっけなく落城した (大坂夏の陣)。

　大坂城落城後、徳川幕府は西日本の大名を監視するために大坂城を天下普請によって再建する。まず豊臣大坂城の焼け跡に盛り土をして土台を築き、藤堂高虎の進言により石垣の高さと堀の幅を豊臣時代の倍にすることに決定する。その結果、石垣の高さは30mを超えた。また天守は豊臣時代の1.5倍の高さの白壁の天守で、本丸には巨大な三重櫓が建ち並んだ (いずれも焼失)。

　この徳川再建大坂城が現在の「大阪城」*である。天守台には昭和6年 (1931) に、豊臣時代の天守をモデルにした模擬天守が建てられた。

*本書では、江戸末期までは「坂」、廃藩置県で大阪府になった明治以降は「阪」と記す。

Edo Castle
(Chiyoda, Tokyo)

Tenshu of Edo Castle (Kan-ei period)
江戸城寛永天守 復元図

Edo Castle, in central Tokyo, was the residence and seat of power of the Edo Shogun. The castle was established in 1457 by Ota Dokan (1432-86). Tokugawa Ieyasu entered Edo in 1590, having been awarded the city and the seven counties of the Kanto region from Toyotomi Hideyoshi. Invested as Shogun in 1603, Ieyasu employed the *Tenkabushin* system to enforce various *daimyo* to assist in the expansion of Edo Castle.

During Ieyasu's time, the *honmaru*, *ni-no-maru*, and *nishi-no-maru* and a huge 48m high white-walled *tenshu* were constructed. Ieyasu's son, the second Shogun, Tokugawa Hidetada (1579-1632) had the tower keep rebuilt on his ascension to power, and his son, Iemitsu (1604-51), the third Shogun, had it rebuilt yet again as a 51m high black, copper-plated keep (p. 62). A major fire destroyed this keep in 1657 and it was never rebuilt.

Construction and enlargement of Edo Castle continued until 1636 when a section of white wall was completed, encasing the *joka-machi* (castle town). The outline of Edo Castle matched that of the modern-day central Chiyoda ward of Tokyo, making it the world's largest castle, far surpassing anything similar in Europe. The current outline of Edo Castle can be found by tracing the 20 *mitsuke* (gates to the castle) through the remaining place names, such as at Akasaka-mitsuke.

江戸城（東京都千代田区）

　江戸城は江戸幕府の将軍の居城である。江戸城ははじめ長禄元年（1457）に太田道灌（1432〜86）が築城。天正18年（1590）に徳川家康が関東7か国の大守として江戸城に入城する。その後、慶長8年（1603）に家康は幕府を開くと、天下普請によって江戸城の拡張にとりかかった。

　家康の時代の江戸城は本丸、二の丸、西の丸が設けられ、本丸に高さ48ｍの白壁の大天守が築かれた。その後、天守は2代将軍秀忠（1579〜1632）と3代将軍家光（1604〜51）の時代に建て替えられ、家光が築いた天守は高さが51ｍで壁は銅板の黒塗りだった（左ページ）。しかしこの天守は明暦3年（1657）の大火で焼失し、それ以降は再建されなかった。

Edo Castle's *honmaru*, *ni-no-maru*, *san-no-maru*, *nishi-no-maru* and the *kita-no-maru* were all arranged within the inner moat. The vast *honmaru* palace served as the living quarters and the political and administrative offices of the shogun. Entry to the inner precincts was via the many gates, including the *Ote-mon*, *Hirakawa-mon*, *Sakashita-mon*, *Kikyo-mon*, *Kita-hanebashi-mon*, *Shimizu-mon*, *Tayasu-mon*, *Hanzo-mon*, and *Sakurada-mon* to name a few. (The *Soto-Sakurada-mon*, *Tayasu-mon* and the *Shimizu-mon* are recognized as Important Cultural Properties.) In 1863, a great fire destroyed the *honmaru*, *ni-no-maru*, and the *nishi-no-maru*, after which the main palace was not rebuilt. Four years later, in 1867, the shogunate collapsed. Control of the nation was returned to the Emperor, who transferred from Kyoto to Edo and turned Tokei Castle into the Imperial Palace.

Among the remains of Edo Castle are the impressive *ishigaki*, including the great *tenshu-dai*, *hori*, *dorui*, four turrets including the three-level *Fujimi-yagura* that replaced the *tenshu* following its destruction by fire, the *Sakurada-tatsumi-yagura*, fifteen gates and the Hyakunin-bansho guard house, so named as it was supposed

　家康の死後も江戸城の普請は続き、寛永13年（1636）に城下町を囲い込む外郭の完成をもって終了した。江戸城の外郭は現在の千代田区とほぼ等しく、当時はヨーロッパの各都市も江戸をしのぐ規模のものはなかった。外郭には江戸市中へ出入りのための門である20の見附が設けられ、赤坂見附など現在の地名に残っているものもある。

　江戸城の内郭（内堀に囲まれたエリア）には、本丸、二の丸、三の丸、西の丸、北の丸などが配されている。本丸には将軍の政務と生活の場である広大な本丸御殿があった。主な門としては、大手門、平川門、坂下門、桔梗門、北桔橋門、清水門、田安門、半蔵門、外桜田門などがある。幕末の文久3年（1863）の火災で本丸、二の丸、

Edo Castle's Sakurada-Tatsumi-Yagura
江戸城桜田巽櫓

to house 100 guards at the entrance to the *honmaru*. The *honmaru*, *ni-no-maru* and part of the *san-no-maru* are open to the public as the Imperial Palace East Gardens, and parts of the *nishi-no-maru* can be visited on special general visitor permits.

西の丸が焼失し、本丸御殿は再建されなかった。慶応3年(1867)に江戸幕府が倒れると、明治天皇が京より行幸し、東京城と改められ、皇居となっている。
　江戸城に残る遺構は、天守焼失後に天守の代わりとなった三重の富士見櫓や桜田巽櫓など4基の櫓と、15棟の門、本丸への検問所となった百人番所などの建築のほか、内堀、天守台をはじめとした石垣、土塁もよく保存されている。本丸、二の丸、三の丸の一部が皇居東御苑として公開され、西の丸の一部も「皇居一般参観」として手続きをすれば参観することができる。

Nagoya Castle
(Nagoya, Aichi)

Tenshu of Nagoya Castle (Before destruction by fire)
名古屋城天守(焼失前)実測図

Nagoya Castle is a large *hirajiro*. Its *ni-no-maru* precinct was the site of the Muromachi period Nagoya Castle where Oda Nobunaga spent his childhood. Nobunaga moved his headquarters to Kiyosu Castle, some 6km northwest, in 1555.

In 1609, Tokugawa Ieyasu ordered the construction of a large castle to be commanded by his ninth son, Yoshinao (1600-50). He chose Nagoya as the location. This new castle was constructed to restrain the western based *daimyo*, especially those with strong ties to the former ruling Toyotomi clan and Toyotomi Hideyori, based in Osaka Castle.

Construction of Nagoya Castle commenced in 1610 under the *Tenkabushin* system, mobilizing twenty *daimyo*, including Kiyomasa Kato. Extensive *ishigaki*, the quality of which surpassed those of Osaka Castle, were completed in just six months. The huge five-story *tenshu*, completed in 1612, was three times the volume of Osaka's. The scale overwhelmed even the Toyotomi clan, clearly stating the authority of the Tokugawa. The magnificent *tenshu* was topped by two golden-scaled *shachi* decorative roof ornaments. Until Nagoya Castle, golden *shachi* roof ornaments had been merely covered in thin gold foil. Nagoya Castle's *shachi* were the first to be made from solid gold, further enhancing its prestige.

名古屋城（愛知県名古屋市）

名古屋市街の中心に位置する巨大な平城。室町時代には那古野城という城が現在の名古屋城二の丸付近にあり、この城で織田信長は幼少期を過ごした。信長は弘治元年（1555）に那古野城の北西6kmにある清洲城へ移った。

慶長14年（1609）、徳川家康は、九男の義直（1600〜50）の居城として、名古屋に新たな城の築城を命じる。この築城は、大坂城にある豊臣秀頼と、豊臣氏に恩のある西国大名を牽制するためのものだった。翌慶長15年から始まった工事は天下普請で行われ、加藤清正をはじめとした西国の諸大名20家が動員された。半年後には大坂城をしのぐ壮大な石垣が完成し、慶長17年には五重の天守が完成する。名古屋天守の容積は大坂城天守の3倍ある巨大なもので、徳川氏の権勢が豊臣氏

Tokugawa Yoshinao entered the *honmaru goten* palace in 1615, but two years later, upon completion of the *ni-no-maru* palace, transferred his residence there. The *honmaru goten* would be reserved solely for the use of the shogun on his visits between Edo and the imperial capital, Kyoto. However, the *honmaru goten* was only used by the second Shogun Hidetada and the third Shogun Iemitsu. By the Meiji period, the palace had been vacant for almost 200 years.

Unfortunately, during the wartime air-raids of 1945, the enormous *tenshu* and golden *shachihoko*, the superb *honmaru goten*, most *yagura* and *mon* were all destroyed by firebombing.

Nagoya Castle *Honmaru* (Before destruction by fire)
名古屋城本丸（焼失前）

を圧倒していることを天下に知らしめた。また、天守の最上層の屋根の上には黄金製の鯱を置いて高い格式を示した。

　元和元年（1615）に徳川義直が本丸御殿に入り、2年後には二の丸御殿が完成した。義直は二の丸で暮らすようになり、本丸は将軍が来訪した際の宿舎とされた。しかし3代将軍の家光を最後に将軍が来訪することはなくなり、本丸は空き家のまま明治維新を迎えた。

　そして昭和20年（1945）の空襲によって、天守が炎上、焼失。本丸御殿・櫓・城

The *tenshu* was rebuilt in reinforced concrete in 1959. Authentic restoration of the *honmaru goten* commenced in 2009 and completed in stages, with the entire palace set for completion in 2018.

Only the *honmaru*'s *seinan*, the *tonan sumi-yagura*, and the *ofuke-maru*'s *seihoku sumi-yagura*, also known as the *kiyosu-yagura* survived. The *kiyosu-yagura*, is so named as it was constructed using the remains of Kiyosu Castle's *tenshu*, and is the largest existing *sanju-yagura*. Nagoya Castle's extensive *ishigaki*, vast moat system, enormous *tenshu* and superb design made it one of Japan's most outstanding *hirajiro* castles.

Nagoya Castle's *Seinan Sumi-Yagura*
名古屋城西南隅櫓

門なども失われた。現在の天守は昭和34年（1959）に外観を復元した鉄筋コンクリート造り。本丸御殿は平成21年（2009）から木造による復元工事が始まり、順次、内部が公開されている。全体の完成と公開は2018年だ。

現存する建物は、本丸の西南隅櫓・東南隅櫓、御深井丸の清洲櫓（西北隅櫓）など。御深井丸の清洲櫓は清洲城天守を移築した三重櫓で、他の現存の三重天守を上回る巨大さを誇る。名古屋城は高い石垣や広大な堀など、完成された平城の姿を伝える、日本屈指の名城といえる。

Nijo Castle
(Nakagyo, Kyoto) ✤

Nijo Castle is a *hirajiro* built in the center of Kyoto by Tokugawa Ieyasu in 1602. It was completed the following year in time for the rituals and celebrations of Ieyasu's investment ceremony by the emperor as shogun. Since that time, Nijo Castle served as the shogun's official lodgings in the capital, and the venue for political rituals staged in Kyoto.

The modern day Nijo Castle has the western positioned *honmaru* surrounded by the *ni-no-maru* in a *rinkaku-shiki nawabari* layout, however, at the time of its construction, it occupied only the current *ni-no-maru* precinct. The castle was redeveloped in 1626 on the occasion of the visit to Nijo Castle by the Emperor Gomizuno-o (reigned 1611-29). The Emperor was married to Masako, the daughter of the second Shogun, Hidetada.

Nijo Castle featured a five-story *tenshu*, which had been relocated from Fushimi Castle and from which the emperor enjoyed the view of Kyoto from the top. The *tenshu* was destroyed by lightning in 1750, and only the *tenshu-dai* stone base remains.

Today, the most admired aspect of Nijo Castle is the *ni-no-maru goten* palace. The various buildings stand connected from

---

二条城（京都市中京区）✤

　徳川家康が京都市街の中心に築いた平城。慶長7年（1602）に築城が開始され、翌年の完成間もない城内で、家康の征夷大将軍宣下（天皇が将軍を任命する）の祝賀儀式が執り行われた。以来、二条城は徳川将軍の上洛の際の宿所とされ、京都における政治的儀礼の場となった。

　現在の二条城は、西側にある本丸を二の丸が囲む輪郭式の縄張だが、家康が築

©iba/PIXTA（ピクスタ）

城した当時は二の丸部分だけだった。それが拡張されたのは、寛永3年（1626）に催された後水尾天皇（在位1611～29）の行幸に際してである。天皇の二条城への行幸は2代将軍秀忠の娘和子が後水尾天皇に嫁いでいた縁によるものであった。本丸には伏見城から移築された五重の天守がそびえ、天皇は最上階に上って京都の街並みを楽しんだという。この天守は寛延3年（1750）に落雷によって焼失した。

Himeji Castle
(Himeji, Hyogo) ❖ ●

Situated on 45.6m high Mt. Hime is Himeji Castle. The white-plastered main tower complex is said to resemble a white egret taking flight, hence Himeji Castle's other name of Shirasagi-jo (lit. White Egret Castle). Himeji Castle has the most remaining original structures. The main *tenshu* surrounding *kotenshu* sub-keeps and connecting *watari-yagura* are National Treasures, while seventy-four other structures are registered as Important Cultural Properties. Along with Horyu-ji Temple (Nara), Himeji Castle became Japan's first World Heritage Site in 1993.

The Battle of Sekigahara in 1600 saw the enforced relocations and re-distribution of *daimyo* fiefs, and a surge of castle construction then commenced. Himeji Castle and Matsue Castle (p. 80) are representative of this movement. Tokugawa Ieyasu gave Harima (southwest Hyogo) to his son-in-law, Ikeda Terumasa (1564-1613), and ordered the expansion and strengthening of the castle.

Work on Himeji Castle's symbolic white *tenshu* commenced in 1601, and was completed in 1609. It is a *hirayama-jiro* and has the largest remaining Edo period built *tenshu*, standing 31.5m high, on top of a 14.8m-high stone base. The uppermost floor of the

姫路城（兵庫県姫路市）❖ ●

　姫路城は標高45.6ｍの姫山に築かれた平山城。白壁の天守群がまるで翼を広げた白鷺のような美しい姿であることから「白鷺城」の美称がある。江戸時代の城郭建築をもっとも多く残している城であり、大天守1棟ほか小天守、渡櫓を含む7棟が国宝、現存建物74棟が重要文化財に指定されている。また、平成5年（1993）に奈良の法隆寺などとともに日本で最初の世界文化遺産に登録された。

　慶長5年（1600）の関ヶ原の戦いののち、大名の全国的な配置替えが行われ、築

城大盛況期を迎える。姫路城や松江城 (p. 80) はこの時期に造られた代表的な大名の城である。徳川家康の娘婿である池田輝政 (1564〜1613) が播磨一国52万石の大名として入封、8年がかりで現在の姫路城を築く。姫路城の象徴である白壁の大天守は慶長14年 (1609) に竣工。五重6階地下1階、天守台の高さは14.8 m、大天守の高さは31.5 mで、江戸時代以前に造られた現存天守のなかで最大である。大天守に、西小天守、乾小天守、東小天守の3つの小天守が渡櫓でロの字形につながれた

Features of a *Tenshu*
姫路城天守の意匠

1. *Shachi*
2. *Irimoya-hafu*
3. *Kara-hafu*
4. *Chidori-hafu*
5. *Hiyoku-irimoya-hafu*
6. *Ishi-otoshi*
7. *Koshimado*

①鯱　②入母屋破風　③唐破風
④千鳥破風　⑤比翼入母屋破風
⑥石落　⑦格子窓

tenshu features *shoin-zukuri* architecture, indicating the formality of the structure. The *tenshu* complex consists of the *daitenshu* (large tower keep) connected by corridor-like *watari-yagura* to the western, northwestern and eastern sub tower keeps, creating a box-like configuration surrounding a small central courtyard. Approaching enemies could be observed from within the main *tenshu* and attacked via the many windows and *teppo-zama* or *ishi-otoshi*.

Himeji Castle was surrounded by a *sotobori* (outer moat) with a circumference of 11.5km, a *nakabori* (central moat) and an *uchi-bori* (inner moat). The JR Himeji Station is where the *sotobori* and main gate once were. From here to the *tenshu* required the breaching of nineteen gates along a confusing maze-like layout. The remaining parts of the magnificent Himeji Castle are all contained within the *uchibori*, from the *uchi-kuruwa* on in.

連立式天守の形式になっている。大天守は初重から五重へと段階的に平面が狭まってゆき、屋根の軒先を結ぶと山のような線を描く。大天守内部は近づく敵を攻撃するための鉄砲狭間や石落の構造を観察することができる。最上階は書院造の様式を取り入れてあり、大天守の格式の高さを示している。外堀・中堀・内堀が取り巻き、外堀の総延長は11.5kmに及んだ。現在のJR姫路駅が外堀と城門のあったところだ（天守から約1km）。現在の姫路城は内堀の内側にあたる「内曲輪」の部分が残っている。

Himeji Castle
姫路城

1. *Tenshu*
2. *Honmaru*
3. *Ni-no-maru*
4. *San-no-maru*
5. *Nishi-no-maru*

①天守 ②本丸 ③二の丸
④三の丸 ⑤西の丸

Matsue Castle
(Matsue, Shimane) ◉

Atop Mt. Kameda on the northern banks of Lake Shinji is Matsue Castle, built by Horio Yoshiharu and his son Tadauji, following their meritorious deeds during the Battle of Sekigahara in 1600. Work commenced in 1607 and was completed five years later. Horio Tadauji died without an heir, and the Horio clan ended in 1611. The Kyogoku clan succeeded and Matsudaira Naomasa (1601–66), a grandson of Tokugawa Ieyasu whose descendants ruled until the end of the feudal period, was made lord of Matsue.

Matsue Castle is a *hirayama-jiro* and its tower is a fine example of an Edo period *tenshu* with four levels, five floors, and an underground basement. Access is via the *tsuke-yagura*, through the basement. The *boro-gata tenshu* has two levels under an *irimoya* roof, and a tower section raised on top. The exterior of the lower sections are covered in black *shitami-ita*, giving the castle an older appearance. In 2015, Matsue Castle's *tenshu* was designated as a National Treasure.

松江城（島根県松江市）●

宍道湖の北岸にある亀田山に築かれた平山城。慶長5年（1600）の関ヶ原の戦いで戦功があった堀尾吉晴（1543〜1611）と忠氏（1577〜1604）の親子は出雲（島根県）を与えられ、松江に新たに城を築くことを決定。築城は慶長12年（1607）に開始され、あしかけ5年の歳月を費やして完成した。堀尾家が断絶した後、京極氏を経て、徳川家康の孫の松平直政（1601〜66）が入城し、明治維新まで松平氏が城主となった。

松江城は築城当時の天守が現存する。天守は四重5階、地下1階で、地下に入口をもつ付櫓が付属する。二重目に入母屋の大屋根をかけ、その上に望楼を載せた望楼型天守。外壁は初重・二重・付櫓を下見板張にしており、黒っぽい古風な外観を呈している。平成27年（2015）に国宝に指定された。

Goryokaku
(Hakodate, Hokkaido)

Hakodate Port on the northern island of Hokkaido was opened to foreign ships in 1854 as part of the Treaty of Kanagawa between the United States of America and the Empire of Japan. To defend Hakodate, the shogunate began construction of the star-shaped Goryokaku fortress in 1857, taking seven years to complete. The *nawabari* was designed by Western studies scholar, Takeda Ayasaburo. The five star-points were designed to allow greater numbers of artillery emplacements while eliminating any blind spots. To avoid becoming a target for enemy canon fire, the fortress was bereft of any tall towers or turrets. It was surrounded by *hori* and thick *dorui* to withstand shelling.

At the end of the feudal period, the Tokugawa loyalists occupied the Goryokaku from October 1868, defending it against the imperial forces. The pro-shogunate forces sought to establish independence as the "Republic of Ezo," but this republic was to be short lived. The rebels were forced to surrender in May of the following year. The main structures within the Goryokaku were later demolished, but the Hakodate Magistrate's Office was reconstructed in 2010. The Goryokaku marked the end of castle construction in Japan.

五稜郭（北海道函館市）

　安政元年（1854）に日米和親条約によって箱館（のち「函館」と改称）の開港が決定する。幕府は守備のために安政4年（1857）から五稜郭の築造を開始し、7年をかけて完成。縄張は蘭学者の武田斐三郎が担当し、星形に5つの稜堡（外側に突き出した堡塁）を配置し、さらに堀と土塁をめぐらせている。稜堡は大砲による攻撃で死角をなくすためのもので、敵の大砲の目標にならないように高い櫓は設けなかった。

　慶応4年（明治元年＝1868）、明治新政府への恭順に反対する旧幕府軍は蝦夷地（北海道）に渡り、10月下旬に五稜郭を占拠する。旧幕府軍は「蝦夷共和国」として独立を目指すが、翌明治2年5月に降伏。こうして日本の城の歴史は、幕末に国防のために造られた五稜郭をもって終わる。のちに五稜郭の建物は取り壊されたが、平成22年（2010）に中心建築である箱館奉行所庁舎が復元された。

Chapter 3
Visiting Samurai Castles

第三章

名城をめぐる

Hirosaki Castle
(Hirosaki, Aomori)

Hirosaki Castle is a *hirayama-jiro* on the east side of the Iwaki River terrace, constructed by the Tsugaru clan in 1611. It is unique in that its Edo period triple-circled *hori* and *ishigaki* remains mostly intact. Construction was commenced by Tsugaru Tamenobu (1550-1607) and completed after his death by his son, Nobuhira (1586-1631).

Hirosaki's five-story *tenshu* was struck by lightning and burned down in 1627. The current three-story *sumi-yagura* was a substitute built in 1811 on the south-eastern corner instead of the original *tenshu* site. The change in size and location was due to a lack of finances, and to ease the Shogunate's concerns should a larger structure have been built.

Three original *yagura* also remain, the *tatsumi, hitsuji-saru* and the *ushitora-yagura* in the *ni-no-maru*, and there are five extant gates, the *otemon, higashimon, minamiuchi-mon, higashiuchi-mon,* and *kitamon*. Cherry trees attract over a million people to Hirosaki in spring. In 2015, the *tenshu* was moved to restore the *ishigaki*. Work should be completed within ten years.

弘前城（青森県弘前市）

　弘前城は戦国時代、津軽地方を統一した津軽為信（1550〜1607）が築城を計画し、その子の信枚（1586〜1631）が慶長16年（1611）に完成した。弘前城は、岩木川東岸の段丘に築かれた平山城で、三重にめぐらされた堀や石垣など、築城当時の縄張をとどめる貴重な遺構である。築城当初の5階建ての天守は寛永4年（1627）に落雷によって焼失。文化8年（1811）に三重の隅櫓を天守の代用として造営した。

　建築ではこの天守をはじめ、3つの三重櫓（辰巳櫓、未申櫓、丑寅櫓）と5つの城門（大手門、東門、南内門、東内門、北門）が現存している。平成27年（2015）より本丸の石垣修復のために天守を移動させる工事が行われており、工期は約10年を予定。城跡は弘前公園になっており、桜の名所として賑わう。

Matsumoto Castle
(Matsumoto, Nagano) ●

National Treasure Matsumoto Castle is a *hirajiro* in central Nagano prefecture. Ishikawa Kazumasa (1533?-93) expanded the castle from 1590, but died three years later. His son, Yasunaga, completed the work in 1594, including the five-story, black lacquered *shitami-ita*-clad *tenshu*. It features six floors within, and provides a fine view of Japan's Northern Alps.

The *tenshu* and older *kotenshu* are connected by fortified *watari-yagura* corridors and both feature the so-called *ishi-otoshi* on the corners, indicating its civil war time construction. The southeastern corner's *tsukimi* (moon viewing) *yagura* has little defensive value, alluding to its peace-time construction. It was built by the Matsudaira clan in 1634 for Shogun Iemitsu's planned visit. Unfortunately, the shogun canceled his trip and never saw the extension, nor enjoyed a moon-viewing party there.

Today, the National Treasure *tenshu* complex, *ishigaki* and *hori*, remain. The *masugata kuromon* and *taikomon* gates have been authentically rebuilt.

松本城（長野県松本市）●

長野県中央部の盆地、松本平に築かれた平城。石川数正（1533?～93）が天正18年（1590）に松本に入封し、築城を開始した。数正はその3年後に亡くなり、子の康長が築城を引き継ぎ、文禄3年（1594）に、今に残る国宝の五重の天守が完成したとされる。大天守は内部6階で、最上階からの北アルプスの眺めは雄大である。

天守は外壁の下部を黒漆塗りの下見板張にしており、全体として黒い外観を呈している。天守と小天守は初重の壁に石落を設けているのに対して、約40年後に松平氏によって増築された月見櫓は廻縁を設けた開放的な造りである。実際に使われなかったものの、この違いは、大天守と小天守は乱世に造られ、月見櫓は天下泰平の時代に造られたことを意味している。遺構は、国宝の天守のほか、本丸と二の丸の石垣や堀の一部、三の丸の堀の一部。また、黒門枡形と太鼓門枡形が復元されている。

Kanazawa Castle
(Kanazawa, Ishikawa)

Ishikawa-mon
石川門

One of the most important castles of the Edo period, Kanazawa Castle was ruled by fourteen generations of the Maeda clan, masters of Kaga and Noto Province (Ishikawa prefecture), and Etchu Province (Toyama prefecture). Maeda Toshiie (1538-99),

---

金沢城（石川県金沢市）

　金沢は、加賀・能登（石川県）、越中（富山県）を領有した、江戸時代最大の大名である前田家の城下町である。天正11年（1583）に前田利家（1538〜99）が金沢に入り、本格的に築城を開始。犀川と浅野川に挟まれた台地に築かれた平山城で、南側に本丸を置いて三方に曲輪を広げた梯郭式の縄張である。

　天正14年（1586）頃に天守が完成したが、慶長7年（1602）に落雷によって焼失し、以降は再建されなかった。石垣、堀などの遺構のほか、建築は重要文化財の石

the richest warlord second only to Tokugawa Ieyasu, further developed the castle. Kanazawa Castle is a *hirayama-jiro* on a plateau between the Sai and Asano Rivers, *teikaku-shiki* in design with the *honmaru* surrounded by the various *kuruwa*.

The large *tenshu*, completed around 1586, was destroyed by lightning in 1602 and never rebuilt. The *hori* and *ishigaki* are original. Both the *masugata*-styled *ishikawa-mon* and a long warehouse called Sanjikken-nagaya are Important Cultural Properties.

The three-story *hishi* (diamond) *yagura*, so named as it is built in a diamond-shaped floor plan, is joined by the corridor-like *gojikken-nagaya* to the *hashizume-mon-tsuzuki-yagura*, another three-story watchtower and command center were reconstructed in 2001. The *kahoku-mon* was reconstructed in 2010, and the *hashizume-mon-ni-no-mon* and Gyokusen'in-maru gardens were restored in 2015.

Southeast of the castle grounds is the Kenroku-en, one of Japan's "top three" *daimyo* gardens along with Mito's Kairaku-en, and Okayama's Koraku-en, famed for its year-round beauty, especially its superb snowscape. The fifth lord, Maeda Tsunanori (1643-1724) began work on the gardens, which continued for 170 years.

川門と三十間長屋が現存する。平成13年(2001)に菱櫓・五十間長屋・橋爪門続櫓、平成22年(2010)に河北門、平成27年(2015)に橋爪門二の門、玉泉院丸庭園などが復元されている。金沢城の南東側に付随する兼六園は、大きな池を中心とした回遊式庭園。水戸の偕楽園、岡山の後楽園とならんで「日本三名園」に数えられる大名庭園で、特に雪吊が美しい。第5代藩主の前田綱紀(1643～1724)が作庭を始め、以後、約170年の歳月を費やして完成した。

Inuyama Castle
(Inuyama, Aichi) ●

National Treasure Inuyama Castle is a *hirayama-jiro* strategically positioned on an 85m-high wedge-shaped mountain. Guarded by the natural moat of the wide, fast-flowing Kiso River, it provides a fine view of the surrounding Nobi Plains. The castle, also known as Hakutei Castle, was constructed in 1537 by Oda Nobunaga's uncle, Oda Nobuyasu (?-1544). The Edo period saw Inuyama go through a succession of masters.

After Tokugawa Ieyasu's ninth son, Yoshinao became the lord of Owari and Nagoya Castle, his administrative adviser, Naruse Masanari (1567-1625) was installed there in 1617. The Naruse clan maintained Inuyama until well after the Meiji Restoration.

Inuyama Castle has a four-story *boro-gata tenshu* with a small two-story basement below, and connected *tsuke-yagura*. It is considered the oldest of the twelve remaining *tenshu* across Japan, and it is believed that the *tenshu*'s *kara-hafu* and the watch tower balcony were added during the Naruse years.

犬山城（愛知県犬山市）●
木曽川の南岸、標高約85mの崖上に築かれた平山城で、濃尾平野が眼下に広がる。別名は白帝城。織田信長の叔父である織田信康（?～1544）が天文6年（1537）に築城したとされる。その後、徳川家康九男の徳川義直が尾張藩主（名古屋城主）となると、付家老とされた成瀬正成（1567～1625）が犬山城主として入城し、成瀬氏が代々城主を務めて明治維新を迎えた。

建築の遺構は国宝の天守のみである。天守は望楼型で、三重4階、地下2階。付櫓が付属する。天守の建立時期は慶長元年（1596）頃と考えられ（諸説あり）、日本に現存する12天守のうち最古のものとされる。天守の唐破風と望楼部分の廻縁は成瀬氏が城主になって以降に改築された。

Hikone Castle
(Hikone, Shiga) ●

Hikone Castle is one of the only five National Treasure castles. The Omi area was originally governed by Ishida Mitsunari from nearby Sawayama Castle. After the Battle of Sekigahara, Tokugawa Ieyasu gave the strategically important lands of Omi

---

彦根城（滋賀県彦根市）●
　琵琶湖の東岸に接した彦根山に築かれた平山城。徳川家康の重臣である井伊直政（1561〜1602）が、慶長5年（1600）の関ヶ原の戦いののちに、近江に18万石を与えられて石田三成の居城であった佐和山城に入る。直政の没後、子の直継（直勝、1590〜1662）が、佐和山城の西方約1kmの彦根山に築城を開始。直継の弟の直孝（1590〜1659）が彦根藩主になると築城を受け継いで元和8年（1622）に完成した。以来、井伊家が城主として明治維新を迎えた。

to General Ii Naomasa (1561-1602). Naomasa died in 1602 of injuries sustained at Sekigahara, leaving work on the *hirayama-jiro* to his sons. Due to Sawayama's inconvenient location, war-torn condition, and mostly because of its association with the despised Ishida Mitsunari, his first son Naotsugu (or Naokatsu, 1590-1662) opted to construct a new castle on Mt. Hikone, 1km from Sawayama on the east banks of Lake Biwa. Hikone castle was completed by the second son Naotaka (1590-1659) in 1622 and held by the Ii clan until Japan's feudal period ended when the shogunate collapsed, and power reverted to the Emperor.

Along with the main *tenshu*, a number of buildings and structures classified Important National Cultural assets remain, including the *nishi-no-maru-sanju-yagura*, the *tenbin-yagura*, *taiko-mon*, and the *ni-no-maru-sawaguchi-tamon-yagura*. The three-story *tenshu* features eighteen *hafu*, the most of any original-condition keep. The upper floors' *mawarien* (railed balcony) the impressive *kara-hafu* roof elements and decorative *kato-mado* windows are also worth noting.

The extensive *daimyo* garden called Genkyu-en below the mountain is beautiful year round, and features a number of traditional buildings.

主郭である彦根山を取り巻くように内堀・中堀・外堀がめぐらされ、堀と堀の間に武家屋敷と町家を配置するという総構の縄張である。石垣や堀などの遺構がよく残り、建築は天守をはじめ、西の丸三重櫓、太鼓門、天秤櫓、二の丸佐和口多門櫓など数多い。国宝の天守は慶長11年(1606)の完成で三重3階。破風が18も設けられており、現存天守のうち最多。破風のほか、上部が火炎形をした華頭窓、唐破風に施された飾り金具、最上階に設けられた高欄付きの廻縁など華麗な外観が特徴である。山麓の大名庭園・玄宮園も見どころだ。

Okayama Castle
(Okayama)

Okayama Castle is a *hirayama-jiro* built *teikaku-shiki* style on a low hill overlooking the Okayama Plains. One of the Great Castles of the Edo Period, it is known as "*U-jo*" (lit. Crow Castle) because of its black lacquered *shitami-ita* walls.

Ukita Hideie (1573-1655) completed Okayama Castle under the instruction of Toyotomi Hideyoshi in 1597. The six-floor *boro-gata tenshu* is a unique shape. The lower two floors are pentagonal, built to fit the rocky outcrop it sits upon. Large and imposing from the front and back, from the sides, it is tall, and narrow. The *boro-gata tenshu* is a large *irimoya*, hip-and-gable roof structure, topped with a watchtower, and is said to resemble Oda Nobunaga's famed Azuchi Castle.

In 1945, the *honmaru* was destroyed by WWII aerial bombings. It was rebuilt in concrete, and provides a great view of the surrounding city, and of the splendid 17th century Koraku-en *daimyo* garden too.

岡山城（岡山市）

　岡山平野の低い丘陵に築かれた平山城。天守は下見板張の外観が特徴で「烏城」とも呼ばれる。宇喜多秀家(1573〜1655)が豊臣秀吉の指導のもとに築城した。岡山は城が築かれた丘陵の名で、そのまま城下町の名となった。

　秀家が建てた天守は、慶長2年(1597)に完成。天守台が不等辺五角形なのが大きな特徴である。この天守台に大きな入母屋屋根をもつ建物を建て、入母屋屋根に望楼を載せた形式にしている。織田信長が築いた安土城の天主に倣ったものといわれ、幻となった安土城の姿を彷彿させる天守であった。

　しかし昭和20年(1945)に空爆によって焼失し、現在の天守は外観を復元した鉄筋コンクリート造りのもの。眺望がすばらしく、旭川を挟んで北側にある後楽園は、17世紀末に造営された回遊式の大名庭園である。

Hiroshima Castle
(Hiroshima)

Mori Terumoto (1553-1625) founded the *hirajiro,* Hiroshima Castle, also known as "*Ri-jo*" (lit. Carp Castle) on a small island in the Otagawa River flowing into Hiroshima Bay.

The Mori clan were ousted following the Battle of Sekigahara in 1600, and transferred to Suo-Nagato (Yamaguchi prefecture). Fukushima Masanori (1561-1624) was then awarded Hiroshima for his actions at Sekigahara, but was later dimissed. In his place, from 1619 until the end of the Edo period, the Asano clan were castellans of Hiroshima Castle.

The large and imposing five-story *boro-gata tenshu* was completed in 1592, but was destroyed in the atomic bombing of 1945. It was reconstructed in concrete in 1958, symbolizing the rebirth of the devastated city. The *ni-no-maru-omote-gomon* gate, *hira-yagura, tamon-yagura* and the *taiko-yagura* have recently been authentically reconstructed.

広島城(広島市)

広島湾に注ぐ太田川の中州に築かれた平城。別名は「鯉城」。中国地方を領有した毛利輝元(1553〜1625)が天正17年(1589)から10年をかけて完成させた。慶長5年(1600)、輝元が関ヶ原の戦いののちに周防・長門(山口県)へ減封されると、福島正則(1561〜1624)が入城して城を拡張。その正則も元和5年(1619)に改易されてしまい、かわって浅野氏が入り、明治維新まで城主となった。

輝元が建てた五重5階の望楼型天守は文禄元年(1592)頃に完成し、昭和20年(1945)まで現存していたが、広島に投下された原爆の爆風によって倒壊した。天守は昭和33年(1958)に外観を復元した鉄筋コンクリート造りで再建され、平成に入ってから二の丸の表御門、平櫓、多門櫓、太鼓櫓などが復元されている。

Marugame Castle
(Marugame, Kagawa)

Marugame Castle is a *hirayama-jiro* on 66m high Mt. Kameyama, facing the Seto Inland Sea. Three tiers of high, unusually shaped and various styled *ishigaki* encircle the mountain in a *rinkaku-shiki* layout. The *honmaru* is located at the top, the *ni-no-maru* east of that, the *san-no-maru* on the hillside, and at the base, surrounding the complex, the *obi-kuruwa* (incidentally, an *obi* is the sash worn around the waist with a kimono). *Mizu-bori* water moats encircle the castle grounds.

In 1642 Yamazaki Ieharu was permitted to rebuild Marugame Castle. Yamazaki had learned *ishigaki* techniques in the 1620's reconstruction of Osaka Castle, but died before finishing Marugame. The succeeding Kyogoku clan oversaw its completion in 1644, and remained at Marugame until the end of the Edo period. It is the smallest of the remaining twelve original *tenshu*.

Along with the *tenshu*, the *ote-ichi-no-mon* gate and *ote-ni-no-mon* remain in original condition, and are listed as Important Cultural Properties. Marugame Castle's *ishigaki* consists of variations of construction types, including *nozura-zumi*, *uchikomi-hagi*, *kirikomi-hagi* and others.

丸亀城（香川県丸亀市）

香川県中西部、瀬戸内海に面した丸亀市はうちわの産地として知られる。丸亀城は、市街地の南に位置する標高66mの亀山に築かれた平山城。山麓から山頂まで3段に重なる高石垣を築いて、山頂に本丸、本丸の東に二の丸、山腹に三の丸、山麓に帯曲輪を配する。亀山の周りに水堀をめぐらせている。

山崎家治（1594～1648）が寛永19年（1642）に着工を始めたが、完成を見ることなく病死し、あとを継いで城主となった京極氏が完成させ幕末に至った。天守は正保元年（1644）頃の完成。天守は現存12天守のうちで規模がもっとも小さい。天守のほかに大手一の門、大手二の門などが現存し、重要文化財。丸亀城の魅力である石垣は、野面積、打込接、切込接などさまざまな種類の石垣を見ることができる。

Kochi Castle
(Kochi)

Yamauchi Katsutoyo was given Tosa Domain, and commenced building a fine *hirayama-jiro* and residence there. Kochi Castle's *nawabari* makes fine use of the lay of the land. The *honmaru* is situated on a southern rise, and at roughly the same elevation, the opposite hill is occupied by the *ni-no-maru*. The *san-no-maru* lies to the east, and to the west, the *nishi-no-maru*.

Many of the central structures were damaged by fire in 1727. The rebuilt *tenshu* was modeled on the original four-level, six-floor *boro-gata* tower, with *mawari-en* balcony and railing. Kochi Castle is particularly historically valuable, being the only castle with all original *honmaru* structures still existing. Fifteen National Important Cultural Properties remain, including the *tenshu*, the Kaitokukan *honmaru-goten*, *tamon-yagura*, *yaguramon*, *dobei*, the *tsumemon,* and the *otemon*.

高知城（高知市）

　山内一豊（1545〜1605）が、土佐（高知県）一国を与えられて築城した平山城。縄張は、城山の山頂部南側に本丸を置き、その北にほぼ同じ高さの二の丸が並び、二の丸の東側の山腹に三の丸、西側の山麓に西の丸を配している。

　享保12年（1727）の火災によって天守を含む建物の大部分が焼失し、26年をかけて再建した城の姿が現在の高知城である。現存する四重6階の天守は、山内一豊の建てた天守に倣ったもので、再建当時としては古風な望楼型の廻縁をめぐらせた天守である。天守をはじめ本丸御殿（懐徳館）、多門櫓、櫓門、土塀など、本丸の建物がそろって現存する唯一の例として貴重であり、ほかに本丸と二の丸をつなぐ詰門、追手門など計15棟が重要文化財に指定されている。

Uwajima Castle
(Uwajima, Ehime)

Uwajima City is famous for pearls, bullfighting, and for Uwajima Castle. Protected north and west by sea, and by *hori* to the south and east, it is both a *yamajiro*, positioned on an 80m-high mountain, and an *umijiro* (sea castle) with ships once entering the moats from the sea. Master castle architect Todo Takatora designed Uwajima Castle in 1596, taking advantage of the coastal terrain to create a pentagonal *nawabari* layout with remarkable defensive capabilities.

The three-story *soto-gata tenshu* built by the succeeding Date clan in 1665 sits directly on mountain bedrock. Decorative *chidori-hafu* above the second floor improve the *tenshu*'s looks, but obstruct the window firing positions, hindering defense.

Besides the *tenshu*, the southern approaches' *karamete* rear *Nobori-tachi-mon* gate and the former *Yamazato-soko* armory (now used as a regional museum) have survived in original condition.

宇和島城（愛媛県宇和島市）

愛媛県西南部、宇和海に面した宇和島市は、闘牛や真珠の養殖で有名な町。江戸時代は伊達氏10万石の城下町で、宇和島城は町を見下ろす標高約80mの城山に築かれている。かつては北側と西側が海に面し、東側から南側にかけて堀をめぐらしていた。海城と呼ばれる形式の城である。慶長元年（1596）に城造りの名手として知られる藤堂高虎が築城。海に面する地形を生かした不等辺五角形の縄張である。

現在、山頂に建つ三重3階の天守は、藤堂氏のあとに城主となった伊達氏による再建で、寛文5年（1665）の建立。総塗籠の層塔型天守である。二重目と三重目に千鳥破風を設けて外観を装飾しており、防御性に乏しい。天守のほか、城山南側の搦手（裏口）にある上り立ち門、武器庫であった旧山里倉庫（城山郷土館として利用）などが現存する。

Iyo Matsuyama Castle
(Matsuyama, Ehime)

Iyo Matsuyama is a splendid castle towering over Matsuyama City from 132m-high Mt. Katsu. The *honmaru* is an elongated north-south enclosure, with the *tenshu-kuruwa*, named Hondan, built on upright *ishigaki* in the northern area. The southwestern foot of Mt. Katsu is the *ni-no-maru*, and the *san-no-maru* takes up the south-western hillside.

Kato Yoshiaki (1563-1631) was rewarded with Iyo Province, and castle construction began in 1602, with a five-story *tenshu* erected. The Gamo clan held Iyo Matsuyama from 1627 and completed the *ni-no-maru*. Lightning destroyed the *tenshu* and the Hondan buildings in 1784. Reconstruction of the *renritsu-shiki* (square-ring shaped complex), including the three-story *tenshu*, *ko-tenshu* sub keep, and *sumi-yagura* linked by *watari-yagura* corridors, was completed in 1852.

Of Japan's twelve existing *tenshu*, this is the newest. The *tamon-yagura*, *jomon* and other structures including gardens have been rebuilt in the *ni-no-maru* section, adding to the atmosphere of this fine castle.

伊予松山城（愛媛県松山市）

　伊予松山城は松山市街中心部の勝山（標高132m）にそびえたつ平山城である。山頂の本丸は南北に細長く、本丸北側の本壇（天守曲輪）と呼ばれる石垣の上に天守が建つ。南西の山腹に二の丸、南西の山麓に三の丸を配している。

　加藤嘉明（1563～1631）が慶長7年（1602）から築城を始め、五重の天守などを建立。寛永4年（1627）に蒲生氏が城主になり、二の丸が完成した。天明4年（1784）に落雷によって天守をはじめとした本壇の建物が焼失。現在の天守は嘉永5年（1852）の再建で、大天守、小天守、隅櫓を渡櫓で結んだ連立式天守である。大天守は三重3階、地下1階の層塔型天守。現存12天守のなかでもっとも新しいものである。二の丸は庭園が整備され、多門櫓や城門などが復元されている。

Nakijin Gusuku
(Kunigami, Okinawa) ❖

Within the Amami and Okinawa islands, castles are called *gusuku*. Nakijin Gusuku in Okinawa's main island's mid north Nakijin Village is strategically located on the slopes of a hill, making use of natural defenses, such as a river, steep cliffs and deep valleys to ward off invaders. The sweeping curves of the thick, sturdy, but rough looking *ishigaki* are their most notable features.

Nakijin Gusuku dates back to the 13th century, when Okinawa was separated into the Hokuzan, Chuzan and Nanzan kingdoms. Nakijin Gusuku was the capital of the northern Hokuzan Kingdom, and after a series of battles, the victors installed an administrator in Nakijin Gusuku in the early 17th century. The ruins of Nakijin Gusuku are a sacred place for the people of Okinawa, and ritual performing worshipers visit regularly. Nakijin, Shuri Castle and other *gusuku* became World Heritage Sites in 2000 as so-called Kingdom of Ryukyu Gusuku Sites and Related Properties.

今帰仁城（沖縄県国頭郡今帰仁村）❖

奄美諸島（鹿児島県）や沖縄では城をグスクと呼ぶ。今帰仁城は沖縄本島北部の本部半島にあるグスクで、山の斜面に築かれている。もっとも高いところにある主郭が本丸に相当し、主郭から下へ向かって石垣で囲まれた区画が段状に連なっている。石垣の塁線が曲線を描いているのがグスクの大きな特徴である。

今帰仁城の歴史は13世紀に遡るといわれる。当時の沖縄本島は北山・中山・南山の3つの王国が分立しており、今帰仁城は北山王国の本拠地であった。興亡を経て17世紀初めに今帰仁城は放棄された。その後、今帰仁城は御嶽（祭祀を行う聖城）となり、多くの人々が参拝に訪れる信仰の場となった。平成12年（2000）に首里城（那覇市）などとともに「琉球王国のグスク及び関連遺産群」として世界文化遺産に登録された。

Appendix

Glossary

Shiro-Matsuri Festivals to Visit

付録

用語集

訪ねてみたい城祭り

Glossary | 用語集

Introduction

Azuchi-Momoyama Period

The era in which Oda Nobunaga and his successor Toyotomi Hideyoshi were at the helm of politics. In general, it refers to the approximately 30-year time span between 1573 and 1603. The name of the period, Azuchi-Momoyama, is derived from Azuchi Castle, the residence of Nobunaga, and Hideyoshi's Fushimi (Momoyama) Castle. The culture of this time is referred to as Azuchi-Momoyama, or simply Momoyama culture and is characterized by luxurious artworks painted directly onto gold leaf covered walls and sliding doors.

Daimyo

Powerful feudal lords with extensive hereditary domains and armies of samurai. *Daimyo* of the Sengoku, or Warring States, period are referred to as warlords, while the Edo period feudal lords were known as *daimyo*. The Edo period *daimyo* were given the authority to govern their territories by the shogun (the de facto ruling authority) and in return were subjected to control through the

はじめに

安土桃山時代
あづちももやまじだい

織田信長と、その後継者である豊臣秀吉が政治の実権を握った時代。一般的には1573～1603年のおよそ30年間を指す。安土桃山の名称は、信長の居城の安土城、秀吉の居城の伏見城跡の桃山に由来する。この時代の文化を安土桃山文化もしくは桃山文化と呼ぶ。金箔を用いた豪華な障壁画（戸や襖に描かれた絵画）がその代表。

大名 だいみょう

広大な領地と多くの家来をもつ武士。戦国時代の大領主を戦国大名と呼ぶが、単に大名という場合は江戸時代の大名を指す。江戸時代の大名は将軍（武士の最高権力者）から領地を支配する権限を与えられたが、参勤交代（大名が原則として1年おきに、領地と江戸を往復する制度）などの統制を受けた。

Sankin-kotai system, whereby their families were to remain in Edo and the *daimyo* yearly alternated their residence between their domains and Edo, providing administrative and guard duties at the shogun's castle.

Chapter 1

Kuruwa

Baileys, precincts and compounds that make up the castle grounds. Can also be written as 郭 (*kaku*). At the center of early modern castles is the main *kuruwa*, the *honmaru*, and the subsequent *ni-no-maru* (second) and the *san-no-maru* (third) *kuruwa*. As the pronunciation of the number "four" and "death" are similar, naming a bailey the fourth *kuruwa* was avoided. In this case, if the *kuruwa* was on the western side of the castle, it would be called the *nishi-no-maru*, or if it protruded from another *kuruwa*, it may be called the *de-no-maru*.

It is not actually known if the various precincts were called *kuruwa* during the medieval times or not. Recently, the central compound of a *yamajiro* is known as the *shu-kaku* or *hon-kaku*, and the adjoining precincts *ni-kaku* and *san-kaku*.

第一章

曲輪 くるわ

城を構成する区画。郭とも書く。近世城郭では城の中心の曲輪を本丸、それに続く曲輪を二の丸、三の丸と呼んだ。ただし、四の丸は四が「死」に通じることから、避けられたようだ。その場合、城の西側にあれば西の丸と呼び、ほかの曲輪から出っ張っていれば出の丸などと呼んだ。

いっぽう、中世城郭の曲輪は当時どう呼ばれていたかよくわかっていない。現在は中世に多い山城の中心の曲輪は、主郭あるいは本郭、それに連なる曲輪を二郭、三郭と仮に呼ぶ。

Teppo

Matchlock guns, first brought to Japan by Portuguese sailors arriving at Tanegashima Island (Kagoshima prefecture) in 1543. The guns' firing mechanism included a fuse of smoldering rope, and so the weapons came to be known as *hinawaju* (lit. burning rope guns). In addition to the matchlock, flintlock guns were developed in the West, but were not used in Japan. During the Sengoku period, matchlock guns went into production across Japan, and Oda Nobunaga was credited with introducing the gun as a main battlefield weapon.

Kato Kiyomasa (1562-1611)

Warlord, *daimyo* and castle construction expert of the Azuchi-Momoyama and early Edo periods, Kiyomasa was born in Owari Province (Aichi prefecture). He served Toyotomi Hideyoshi from a young age, and played a major role in many battles, in particular Hideyoshi's Korean invasions of 1592-93 and 1597-98. Kiyomasa was master of Higo Province (Kumamoto prefecture) and following Hideyoshi's death, he allied himself with Tokugawa Ieyasu. Known for his fine

鉄砲 てっぽう

1543年に種子島（鹿児島県）に来航したポルトガル船の船員によってもたらされた鉄砲が、日本へのはじめての伝来という。日本に伝わった鉄砲は発射装置が火縄によるもので、火縄銃と呼ばれた。西洋では火縄銃のほかに、発射装置に鉱石を用いる鉄砲が発達したが、日本では広まらなかった。戦国時代、火縄銃は国内各地で生産されるようになり、織田信長が合戦の主力武器として導入した。

加藤清正 かとうきよまさ
（1562～1611）

安土桃山時代～江戸時代初期の武将、大名。尾張（愛知県）に生まれる。幼少の頃より豊臣秀吉に仕え、多くの合戦で活躍。とくに秀吉による朝鮮出兵（1592～93、1597～98）では朝鮮に渡り、主力として転戦した。秀吉の死後、徳川家康に味方して肥後（熊本県）一国を与えられる。築城の名人として知られ、熊本城を築いたほか、徳川氏による名古屋城の築城に関わっている。

castle architectural skills, he is famed for having built Kumamoto Castle, and the stone bases of Nagoya Castle for the Tokugawa.

Todo Takatora (1556-1630)

Warlord, *daimyo* and castle construction expert of the Azuchi-Momoyama and early Edo periods, Todo Takatora was born in Omi Province (Shiga prefecture). He initially started as a low-ranking *ashigaru* foot-soldier in the service of the Azai clan of Omi. Upon the demise of the Azai, he served a number of lords, including Toyotomi Hideyoshi with distinction, before being awarded Uwajima Castle (Ehime prefecture). Following the passing of Hideyoshi, Takatora served Tokugawa Ieyasu and received Tsu Castle in Ise Province (Mie prefecture). Besides Kato Kiyomasa, Takatora is recognized as the preeminent castle designer and architect. He was also responsible for the design of Ieyasu's most gorgeous mausoleum, the Nikko Toshogu (Tochigi prefecture).

藤堂高虎 とうどうたかとら
(1556〜1630)

安土桃山時代〜江戸時代初期の武将、大名。近江(滋賀県)に生まれる。はじめ近江の浅井氏に仕え、浅井氏滅亡後は主君を変えながらしだいに頭角を現し、豊臣秀吉より宇和島城(愛媛県)を与えられる。秀吉死後は徳川家康に仕え、伊勢(三重県)の津城主となる。加藤清正と並ぶ築城の名人として知られる。徳川家康を祀る日光東照宮(栃木県)の設計も担当した。

Yumi

An instrument with which to launch an arrow. Japanese bows are on average two meters twenty centimeters in length, much longer than modern standard archery bows. Western bows are held and fired from the mid section, while Japanese bows are held and arrows notched from the lower third position. In addition to being a major weapon, the bow is used at shrines for *kyudo* (traditional Japanese archery), the spiritual training of body and mind.

Shikkui

A lime-based plaster used for covering the walls of structures. A similar substance had been used in ancient Egypt as an adhesive in timber construction. In Japan, the *shikkui* stucco plaster consists of a mixture of slaked lime (calcium hydroxide), hemp fibers, a paste made from a type of seaweed and other ingredients. Coatings of *shikkui* were applied to castle walls and to tile joints. It provided the castle with a beautiful, graceful image, and after the Edo period, *shikkui* was also used on private houses.

弓 ゆみ

矢を飛ばすための器具。日本の弓は洋弓（アーチェリー）に比べて長く、約2m20cmが標準。また、洋弓が弓の長さの真ん中あたりに矢をつがえるのに対して、日本の弓は下から3分の1あたりにつがえるのが特徴。日本では、弓は武器として使用されたほか、神社での儀礼用や心身を鍛える武芸（弓道）としても用いられてきた。

漆喰 しっくい

石灰を材料とする建築素材。海外では古代エジプトの時代から建材の接着剤として使われていた。日本における漆喰は、消石灰（水酸化カルシウム）に麻糸や糊（海藻などが原料）などを加えて練ったもの。城では壁の塗装や瓦の目地などに塗られた。白色をしているため外観を美しく見せる効果があり、江戸時代以降は民家にも広く用いられるようになった。

Oda Nobunaga (1534-1582)

Warlord and *daimyo* of the Azuchi-Momoyama period. Born in Owari (Aichi prefecture), he defeated warlord Imagawa Yoshimoto (1519-1560) at the Battle of Okehazama in 1560, greatly expanding his territories and reputation. Nobunaga assisted in raising General Ashikaga Yoshiaki (1537-97) to the position of shogun, but later opposed him, battling against Yoshiaki's Sengoku warlord and Hongan-ji temple religious group supporters. In 1576, Nobunaga built the most magnificent Azuchi Castle on the banks of Lake Biwa in Omi (Shiga prefecture), from where he continued his quest to unify the nation. During a protracted battle against the Mori clan in the central western Chugoku regions, Nobunaga was attacked while at the Honno-ji Temple in Kyoto by his trusted general, Akechi Mitsuhide (1528-82) and killed.

織田信長 おだのぶなが
（1534〜1582）

戦国時代・安土桃山時代の武将、大名。尾張（愛知県）に生まれる。1560年に桶狭間の戦いで戦国大名の今川義元（1519〜60）を破り、勢力を拡大。足利義昭（1537〜97）を援助して将軍に就任させるが、のちに対立。義昭に味方する戦国大名や本願寺などの宗教勢力と抗争をくりひろげる。1576年に近江（滋賀県）の琵琶湖畔に、安土城を築城。天下統一に向けて中国地方の毛利氏などと戦っている最中、本能寺の変で家臣の明智光秀（1528〜82）に襲われて殺された。

Irimoya-zukuri

A form of roofing construction. The top resembles a downward facing opened book, with eves extending in four directions. The uppermost roofs of all castle *tenshu* are of *irimoya-zukuri* gable-and-hip roof style. *Irimoya* also refers to the triangular section and decorative roofing gables known as *hafu*. Besides the *irimoya-hafu*, there is a *chidori-hafu* (plover gable) and a *kara-hafu*, (aristocratic gable). *Chidori-hafu* are roof-mounted triangular gables supporting a section of roofing. *Kara-hafu* feature graceful undulating curves and are used in highly formal structures.

Shoin-zukuri

A style of ruling-class residential architecture based around the *tatami* room, characterized by a recessed writing stall, a raised decorative alcove for displaying scrolls called a *toko,* and another alcove featuring split-level shelving. The style appeared in the late 15th century Muromachi period, and was realized in the Azuchi-Momoyama period. *Shoin* originally referred to the study of temple, and later, official visitor's reception rooms. This style later became the standard design of Japanese homes. The oldest

入母屋造 いりもやづくり

屋根の形式のひとつ。上部は本を伏せたような形をしており、下部は四方向に庇が付いている。天守の最上重の屋根はすべて入母屋造である。また、屋根の両端の部分を破風といい、入母屋造の屋根の両端の三角形部分は入母屋破風という。破風の種類には入母屋破風のほかに千鳥破風、唐破風などがある。千鳥破風は、屋根の斜面に三角形の屋根を載せたもの。唐破風は屋根の端の部分を上に曲げたもので、格式の高い建物に用いられる。

書院造 しょいんづくり

畳敷きの部屋を中心とした、支配者の住宅の建築様式。室町時代中期(15世紀後半)に起こり、安土桃山時代に完成した。書院はもともと寺院の書斎の意味で、支配者の住居に使われるようになって主人と客の公的な対面の場となった。書院造は、床(絵や書を掛ける場所)や、板を左右に食い違いに取り付けた棚などの飾りを設けるのが特徴。以降の日本住宅の基礎となった。現存するもっとも古い書院

surviving example of *shoin-zukuri* architecture can be found at Kyoto's Ginkaku-ji (lit. Silver Pavilion) Togudo Hall.

Toyotomi Hideyoshi (1537-1598)

Warlord and *daimyo* of the Sengoku period. Born to a farmer in Owari (Aichi prefecture). Served Oda Nobunaga, rising in the ranks to become a senior statesman of the Oda clan. Following Nobunaga's assassination at the hands of another trusted general, Akechi Mitsuhide, Hideyoshi was quick to take revenge, and take the helm of Nobunaga's empire, completing the task of conquering the nation. In 1583 he constructed the original Osaka Castle. Hideyoshi then subjugated Shikoku and Kyushu regions, and in 1590, forcing the surrender of the mighty Hojo clan in the Kanto regions, succeeded in national unification. During this time he was made *kanpaku* (regent to the emperor). He set his sights on conquering Korea and sent troops, but failed to take the peninsula before passing away.

造は、京都・銀閣寺の東求堂である。

豊臣秀吉 とよとみひでよし (1537〜1598)

戦国時代・安土桃山時代の武将、大名。尾張（愛知県）に生まれる。農民出身といわれる。織田信長に仕えてしだいに頭角を現し、織田家の重臣のひとりとなる。信長が明智光秀に殺されると、すぐに光秀を破り、天下取りの主導権を握る。1583年、大坂城を築城。その後、四国、九州を平定し、1590年に関東の北条氏を降伏させて全国統一を果たした。この間に関白（天皇を補佐する重職）に就任。晩年に朝鮮に出兵するが失敗に終わる。

Tokugawa Ieyasu
(1542-1616)

Founder of the Edo shogunate. Born the son of the *daimyo* of Mikawa Province (Aichi prefecture). Held hostage by the Oda clan from age six to nine, then from nine to nineteen by the Imagawa clan. Freed with the death of Imagawa Yoshimoto at the Battle of Okehazama, he allied himself with Oda Nobunaga and unified Mikawa. His powers were expanded under Nobunaga, and he submitted to Hideyoshi's growing influence following the death of Nobunaga, accepting the Kanto region from Hideyoshi as his fief and basing himself in Edo Castle. Upon the death of Hideyoshi, the nation was again returned to war status, and in 1600, Ieyasu claimed victory in the decisive Battle of Sekigahara, after which Ieyasu assumed the position of shogun. In 1615, he solidified his authority by attacking Osaka Castle and destroying the last remnants of the rival Toyotomi clan.

徳川家康 とくがわいえやす
(1542〜1616)

江戸幕府の初代将軍。三河(愛知県)の大名の子として生まれる。6歳から19歳まで、織田家や今川家の人質となる。桶狭間の戦いで今川義元の死後、今川家を離れたのちに織田信長と同盟して三河を統一。信長とともに勢力を拡大するが、信長の死後に豊臣秀吉に服従。秀吉の天下統一にともなって関東を領有することとなり、江戸城を居城とする。秀吉の死後、1600年の関ヶ原の戦いで、天下の主導権を握って将軍に就任。1615年に豊臣氏を滅ぼして江戸幕府を盤石のものとした。

Rojo

Preventing the enemy from breaching the castle. Often tactics would dictate the withdrawing into the confines of the castle and waiting for reinforcements. To bring a castle down, the most-often used tactics included *chikara-zeme* (attacking with great force) or those of attrition, such as *hyro-zeme*, which involves the cutting off of vital food supplies and starving the defenders into surrender. If the castle was constructed on lowlands, the flooding of rivers to submerge the castle was also used.

Tatami

A type of floor covering. *Tatami* are made of tightly woven rice straw, covered in finely woven rush grass, and finished with strips of cloth edging. In the Heian period, *tatami* were only placed where people were to sit. From the late Muromachi period, they began to fill entire rooms. It was expected that footwear was to be removed before stepping on *tatami*. Likewise, split toed socks called *tabi* were worn with kimono so as not to taint the *tatami* with bare feet.

籠城 ろうじょう

城の中に入って敵を防ぐこと。籠城することで時間をかせぎ、援軍を待つことも多かった。城を攻める方法は、力づくで城に攻め寄せる「力攻め」と、城への食糧の補給路を断つことによって城内の兵を飢餓状態に陥れる「兵糧攻め」が代表。そのほか、城が低地にある場合、城の周囲に堤防を築き、水をひきいれて水没させる「水攻め」も行われた。

畳 たたみ

敷物（床の上に敷くもの）のひとつ。畳床（ワラを重ねて糸で縫い付けたもの）の表面を、畳表（イグサを編んで作った敷物）でくるみ、縁に帯状の布を縫い付ける。平安時代は人が座る場所だけに畳を敷いたが、室町時代後期から部屋いっぱいに敷き詰めるようになった。畳に上がる場合は履物を脱ぐ。和装で他人の家を訪問する場合、裸足で歩いて畳の表面を汚さないように足袋（和装の靴下）をはくことが一般的。

Furo

Bathroom. Until the early Edo period, most bathing was conducted with buckets of hot water. This type of bathroom is called *yudono*. *Furo* originally referred to steam baths created by boiling water. From the mid Edo period, bath tubs became the norm. Bathrooms were not features of standard housing, and so people would go to public baths during the Edo period.

Chashitsu

Chashitsu are specially designed tea rooms in which to prepare and enjoy green tea. From the Muromachi period, the warrior class adopted a tea culture, whereby hosts would entertain their guests with tea, and so *chashitsu* came to be built. Basic, lightly decorated *chashitsu* were usually four-and-a-half *tatami* mat sized rooms, although three and two mat rooms were also made. Toyotomi Hideyoshi constructed a golden *chashitsu* with the walls and ceiling decorated in gold leaf. With the spread of tea culture, the Sengoku period *daimyo* would collect expensive tea implements.

風呂 ふろ

浴室。江戸時代初期までの入浴は、湯だらいの中で湯を浴びるもので、その部屋を湯殿という。風呂は蒸し風呂（熱湯から発生させた蒸気を浴室に充満させる）を意味したが、江戸中期以降、浴槽に湯をはって入浴するようになった。江戸時代は庶民の家に風呂はなかったため、公衆浴場（風呂屋、銭湯）に出かけて入浴した。

茶室 ちゃしつ

茶（おもに抹茶＝粉末にした緑茶を湯で攪拌した茶）をふるまう専用の部屋。室町時代、主人が客に茶をたててもてなす茶会が武士階級に広まり、茶室が造られるようになった。茶室は四畳半（畳4枚と半分を敷いた部屋）を基本として、三畳、二畳の部屋もある。豊臣秀吉は、壁や天井に金箔を貼った「黄金の茶室」を設けた。また、茶会の流行にともなって、戦国大名たちは高価な茶器を収集した。

Noh Stage

Traditional theatrical 5.5m² stages, with raised wooden flooring for the performing of *Noh* recitals accompanied by music, also *Kyogen* comedy and dance performances. The stages' back wall features a painting of a large pine tree, while the stages' left, front and right sides are opened for viewing the performance. An access corridor leads from the backstage dressing rooms to the left rear corner of the main stage. *Noh* stages were originally erected outdoors, and since the Meiji period (1868-1912), when built indoors, they incorporate roofing.

Kaido

Highways. The Tokugawa maintained five major highway routes commencing from Edo's Nihonbashi: the Tokaido (East Coast Route to Kyoto), the Nakasendo (Inland Mountain Route to Kyoto), the Nikko-kaido (to Nikko, Tochigi prefecture), the Koshu-kaido (to Kofu, Yamanashi prefecture), and the Oshu-kaido (to Shirakawa, Fukushima prefecture). Government approved post towns with inns, shops and checkpoint barriers were located along these strategically and economically vital highways.

能舞台 のうぶたい

日本の古典芸能の能（楽器の演奏にのせ、舞をまじえて物語が進行する演劇）や狂言（語りや舞をまじえた喜劇）を演じるための専用舞台。舞台は一辺約5.5mの正方形で、床は板張り。奥に松を描いた壁があり、前面と左右の三方は開け放している。舞台に向かって左側に、楽屋から舞台へ至るための廊下が設けられている。能舞台は当初は野外に造られたもので、明治以降、屋内に造られる場合でも舞台には屋根をかけている。

街道 かいどう

交通上の主要な陸路。徳川家康は1601年に江戸の日本橋を起点とする五つの街道（五街道）の整備を進めた。五街道は次のとおり。東海道（江戸～京都 ＊太平洋沿いを経由）、中山道（江戸～京都 ＊内陸部を経由）、日光街道（江戸～日光〈栃木県日光市〉）、甲州街道（江戸～甲府〈山梨県甲府市〉）、奥州街道（江戸～白河〈福島県白河市〉）。街道には関所（通行人を管理するための役所）や、宿・商店などが密集する宿場が置かれた。

Spring *Shiro-Matsuri* Festivals to Visit

February

Early February

Hirosaki Castle Snow Lantern Festival
Hirosaki Castle
Hirosaki city, Aomori

Early February - Early March

Odawara Plum Festival
Odawara Castle
Odawara city, Kanagawa

2nd Thursday - Saturday

Morioka *Yuki-akari* Snow Candle Festival
Morioka Castle
Morioka city, Iwate

Late February - March 31

Mito Plum Blossom Festival
Mito Castle
Mito city, Ibaraki

March

Early March

Nagoya Castle Camellia Exhibition
Nagoya Castle
Nagoya city, Aichi

Late March - Early April

Nagoya Castle Spring Festival
Nagoya Castle
Nagoya city, Aichi

Late March - Early April

Fukuoka Castle Sakura Festival
Fukuoka Castle
Fukuoka city, Fukuoka

Late March - Middle April

Oshiro Castle Festival
Matsue Castle
Matsue city, Shimane

ぜひ訪ねてみたい城祭り【春】

- ●2月上旬
  弘前城雪燈籠まつり　弘前城　青森県弘前市
- ●2月上旬～3月上旬
  小田原梅まつり　小田原城　神奈川県小田原市
- ●2月第2木曜～土曜日
  もりおか雪あかり　盛岡城　岩手県盛岡市
- ●2月下旬～3月31日
  水戸の梅まつり　水戸城　茨城県水戸市

- ●3月上旬
  名古屋城つばき展
- ●3月下旬～4月上旬
  名古屋城春の陣　桜まつり
  名古屋城　愛知県名古屋市
- ●3月下旬～4月上旬
  福岡城さくらまつり　福岡城　福岡市
- ●3月下旬～4月中旬
  お城まつり　松江城　島根県松江市

Late March - Middle April

Cherry Blossom Festival
Wakayama Castle
Wakayama city, Wakayama

April

1st Saturday - Sunday

**Inuyama Castle
Spring Festival**
Inuyama Castle
Inuyama city, Aichi

1-15

**Tsuyama
Cherry Blossom Festival**
Tsuyama Castle
Tsuyama city, Okayama

1-20

**Hikone Castle
Cherry Blossom Festival**
Hikone Castle
Hikone city, Shiga

1-20

**Maruoka Castle
Sakura Festival**
Maruoka Castle
Sakai city, Fukui

1-30

**Takato Castle Site Park
Cherry Blossom Festival**
Takato Castle
Ina city, Nagano

1st Friday - Sunday

Oshiro Castle Festival
Iyo Matsuyama Castle
Matsuyama city, Ehime

Early April

**Himeji Castle Cherry Blossom
Viewing Festival /
Cherry Blossom at night**
Himeji Castle　Himeji city, Hyogo

- 3月下旬〜4月中旬
  和歌山城桜まつり　和歌山城　和歌山市
- 4月第1土曜日〜日曜日
  春の犬山お城まつり　犬山城　愛知県犬山市
- 4月1〜15日
  津山さくらまつり　津山城　岡山県津山市
- 4月1〜20日
  彦根城桜まつり　彦根城　滋賀県彦根市
- 4月1〜20日
  丸岡城桜まつり　丸岡城　福井県坂井市
- 4月1〜30日
  高遠さくら祭り　高遠城　長野県伊那市
- 4月第1金曜〜日曜日
  お城まつり　伊予松山城　愛媛県松山市
- 4月上旬
  姫路城観桜会・姫路城夜桜会
  姫路城　兵庫県姫路市

Early April

Kochi Castle Flower Corridor
Kochi Castle
Kochi city, Kochi

Early April

Matsumoto Castle Nighttime Cherry Blossom Viewing
Matsumoto Castle
Matsumoto city, Nagano

Early April

Okazaki Cherry Blossom Festival
Okazaki Castle
Okazaki city, Aichi

Early - Middle April

Ueda Castle Senbon-Zakura Festival
Ueda Castle
Ueda city, Nagano

Middle - Late April

Kaikoen Garden Cherry Blossom Festival
Komoro Castle
Komoro city, Nagano

Early April - Early May

Tsuruga-jo Castle Cherry Blossom Festival
Aizuwakamatsu Castle
Aizuwakamatsu city, Fukushima

12

Takeda Shrine Spring Festival
Tsutsujigasaki Yakata
Kofu city, Yamanashi

Middle April - Early May

Morioka Cherry Blossom Festival
Morioka Castle
Morioka city, Iwate

- 4月上旬
  高知城花回廊　高知城　高知市
- 4月上旬
  松本城夜桜会　松本城　長野県松本市
- 4月上旬
  岡崎の桜まつり　岡崎城　愛知県岡崎市
- 4月上旬〜中旬
  上田城千本桜まつり　上田城　長野県上田市
- 4月中旬〜下旬
  懐古園桜まつり　小諸城　長野県小諸市
- 4月上旬〜5月上旬
  鶴ヶ城さくらまつり　会津若松城
  福島県会津若松市
- 4月12日
  武田神社例大祭　躑躅ヶ崎館　山梨県甲府市
- 4月中旬〜5月上旬
  盛岡さくらまつり　盛岡城　岩手県盛岡市

23-May 5

**Hirosaki
Cherry Blossom Festival**
Hirosaki Castle
Hirosaki city, Aomori

Late April

Ueda Sanada Festival
Ueda Castle
Ueda city, Nagano

Late April - Early May

**Panorama Night View
from Gifu Castle**
Gifu Castle
Gifu city, Gifu

Late April - Late May

**Matsumae
Cherry Blossom Festival**
Matsumae Castle
Matsumae town, Hokkaido

Spring begins in February according to the old Japanese calendar.

●4月23日〜5月5日
　弘前さくらまつり　弘前城　青森県弘前市
●4月下旬
　上田真田まつり　上田城　長野県上田市
●4月末〜5月上旬
　岐阜城パノラマ夜景　岐阜城　岐阜市
●4月下旬〜5月中旬
　松前さくらまつり　松前城
　北海道松前郡松前町

Summer *Shiro-Matsuri* Festivals to Visit

May

3

Odawara Hojo Godai Festival
Odawara Castle
Odawara city, Kanagawa

3-4

Marugame Castle Festival
Marugame Castle
Marugame city, Kagawa

Early May

Kitsuki Castle Festival
Kitsuki Castle
Kitsuki city, Oita

Middle May

Hakodate Goryokaku Festival
Goryokaku
Hakodate city, Hokkaido

Early - Middle May

Azalea Festival at Senshu Park
Kubota Castle
Akita city, Akita

3rd Saturday - Sunday

Sendai Aoba Festival
Sendai Castle
Sendai city, Miyagi

Middle May

Himeji Castle Festival
Himeji Castle
Himeji city, Hyogo

June

1st Sunday

Azuchi Nobunaga Festival
Azuchi Castle
Omi Hachiman city, Shiga

ぜひ訪ねてみたい城祭り【夏】

- ●5月3日
  小田原北條五代祭り
  小田原城　神奈川県小田原市
- ●5月3〜4日
  丸亀お城まつり　丸亀城　香川県丸亀市
- ●5月上旬
  きつきお城まつり　杵築城　大分県杵築市
- ●5月中旬
  箱館五稜郭祭　五稜郭　北海道函館市
- ●5月上旬〜中旬
  千秋公園つつじまつり
  久保田城　秋田市
- ●5月第3土曜〜日曜日
  仙台・青葉まつり 仙台城 宮城県仙台市
- ●5月中旬
  姫路お城まつり　姫路城　兵庫県姫路市
- ●6月第1日曜日
  あづち信長まつり 安土城 滋賀県近江八幡市

1st Friday - Sunday

Kanazawa Hyakumangoku Festival
Kanazawa Castle
Kanazawa city, Ishikawa

Last Saturday - Sunday

Matsumoto Castle Taiko Drum Festival
Matsumoto Castle
Matsumoto city, Nagano

22-24

Himeji Yukata Festival
Himeji Castle
Himeji city, Hyogo

July

Middle July

Summer Night Festival in Kochi Castle
Kochi Castle
Kochi city, Kochi

Middle July - August 31

Panorama Night View from Gifu Castle
Gifu Castle
Gifu city, Gifu

Summer begins in May according to the old Japanese calendar.

- 6月第1金曜〜日曜日
  金沢百万石まつり 金沢城 石川県金沢市
- 6月22〜24日
  姫路ゆかたまつり 姫路城 兵庫県姫路市
- 7月中旬
  高知城・夏の夜のお城まつり
  高知城　高知市
- 7月中旬〜8月31日
  岐阜城パノラマ夜景　岐阜城　岐阜市

- 7月最終土曜〜日曜日
  松本城太鼓まつり
  松本城　長野県松本市

Autumn *Shiro-Matsuri* Festivals to Visit

August

Middle August

Nagoya Castle Summer Festival
Nagoya Castle
Nagoya city, Aichi

September

Middle September

Kochi Castle Autumn Festival
Kochi Castle
Kochi city, Kochi

Late September

Aizu Festival
Aizuwakamatsu Castle
Aizuwakamatsu city, Fukushima

October

Early October

Maruoka Old Castle Festival
Maruoka Castle
Sakai city, Fukui

Early October

Matsushiro Clan Sanada Jumangoku Festival
Matsushiro Castle
Nagano city, Nagano

Middle October - Middle December

Nijo Castle Festival
Nijo Castle
Kyoto city, Kyoto

Late October

Autumn Inuyama Castle Festival
Inuyama Castle
Inuyama city, Aichi

Late October - Early November

Shuri Castle Festival
Shuri Castle
Naha city, Okinawa

ぜひ訪ねてみたい城祭り【秋】

●8月中旬
名古屋城宵まつり 名古屋城 愛知県名古屋市
●9月中旬
高知城・秋のお城まつり
高知城 高知市
●9月下旬
会津まつり 会津若松城 福島県会津若松市
●10月上旬
丸岡古城まつり 丸岡城 福井県坂井市

●10月上旬
松代藩真田十万石まつり
松代城 長野市
●10月中旬～12月中旬
二条城まつり 二条城 京都市
●10月下旬
秋の犬山お城まつり 犬山城 愛知県犬山市
●10月下旬～11月上旬
首里城祭 首里城 沖縄県那覇市

Winter *Shiro-Matsuri* Festivals to Visit

November

3
Matsumoto Citizen's Festival and Matsumoto Castle Festival
Matsumoto Castle
Matsumoto city, Nagano

Early - Middle November
Gujo Hachiman Autumn Leaves Festival
Gujohachiman Castle
Gujo city, Gifu

Early - Middle November
Odawara Castle Chrysanthemum Exhibition
Odawara Castle
Odawara city, Kanagawa

Middle November
Hagi Jidai Festival
Hagi Castle
Hagi city, Yamaguchi

January

1
U-jo Castle *Hatsuyume* Festival
Okayama Castle
Okayama city, Okayama

Late January - Early February
Nakijin Gusuku Cherry Blossom Festival
Nakijin *Gusuku*
Nakijin village, Kunigami, Okinawa

Autumn begins in August and winter begins in November according to the old Japanese calendar.

ぜひ訪ねてみたい城祭り【冬】

- 11月3日
  市民祭松本まつり・お城祭り
  松本城　長野県松本市
- 11月上旬～中旬
  郡上八幡城もみじまつり
  郡上八幡城　岐阜県郡上市
- 11月上旬～中旬
  小田原城菊花展
  小田原城　神奈川県小田原市
- 11月中旬
  萩時代まつり　萩城　山口県萩市
- 1月1日
  烏城初夢まつり
  岡山城　岡山市
- 1月下旬～2月上旬
  今帰仁グスク桜まつり
  今帰仁城　沖縄県国頭郡今帰仁村

三浦正幸 みうら まさゆき

広島大学名誉教授。名古屋出身。東京大学工学部建築学科卒業、工学博士。一級建築士。竪穴式住居（縄文時代）から近代建築（昭和時代）まで、日本の建築の文化財学的調査・設計・復元など全般を研究。設計に岡崎城東隅櫓・浜松城天守門など多数。一般向けの城郭講座や講演も多数行っている。著書・監修に『城のつくり方図典』（小学館）、『すぐわかる日本の城』（東京美術）など。

クリス グレン

オーストラリア出身、名古屋在住。ラジオDJ、タレント、翻訳者、英文ライター、インバウンド観光アドバイザー。戦国史に造詣が深く、訪れた城は550か所以上に及ぶ。NHK WORLD-JAPAN *SAMURAI CASTLES* などテレビ出演も多数。著書に『忍者バイリンガルガイド』（小学館）、『豪州人歴史愛好家、名城を行く』（宝島社）、『The Battle of Sekigahara』（Book Locker）がある。

編集協力
内田和浩

装丁・本文デザイン
金田一亜弥　高畠なつみ（金田一デザイン）